PICTURE FRAMING
BASICS

PICTURE FRAMING
BASICS

Hugh Foster

STERLING PUBLISHING CO., INC.
NEW YORK

Library of Congress Cataloging-in-Publication Data

Foster, Hugh.
    Picture framing basics / Hugh Foster.
       p.   cm.
    Includes index.
    ISBN 0-8069-0646-4
    1. Picture frames and framing.   I. Title.
    N8550.F67   1997
    749′.7—dc21   96-37955
                                 CIP

1   3   5   7   9   10   8   6   4   2

Published by Sterling Publishing Company, Inc.
387 Park Avenue South, New York, N.Y. 10016
© 1997 by Hugh Foster
Distributed in Canada by Sterling Publishing
c/o Canadian Manda Group, One Atlantic Avenue, Suite 105
Toronto, Ontario, Canada M6K 3E7
Distributed in Great Britain and Europe by Cassell PLC
Wellington House, 125 Strand, London WC2R 0BB, England
Distributed in Australia by Capricorn Link (Australia) Pty Ltd.
P.O. Box 6651, Baulkham Hills, Business Centre, NSW 2153, Australia
Manufactured in the United States of America
All rights reserved

Sterling ISBN 0-8069-0646-4

Contents

Acknowledgments 7

Introduction 8

Safety Instructions 9

1 • **Frame Design Considerations** 10

2 • **Picture Frame Components** 15

3 • **Picture-Framing Tools** 17
Miter-Cutting Tools 17; Framing Clamps 25; Miscellaneous Framing Tools 30

4 • **Determining the Amount of Frame Stock Needed** 34

5 • **Choosing Commercial Frames and Moldings** 36
Disassembling a Commercial Picture Frame 40

6 • **Making Moldings** 43
Making Complex Moldings 53

7 • **Cutting and Assembling a Basic Frame** 56
Assembling "Invisible" Wooden Frame Corners 60; Frames You Can Open 63

8 • **Choosing and Cutting Mats** 68
Cutting Mats with the MatMate System 70; Double Matting 73; Cutting Curved Openings in Mats 79

9 • **Selecting and Cutting Glass** 87
Cutting Techniques 87; Using Plexiglas 90

10 • **Assembling and Closing the Work** 92
Assembling a Metal Frame 95

11 • **Hanging Framed Pictures** 105

12 • **Projects** 108
Needlework Project 108; Poster Frame Project 116

Appendices 119

Glossary 121

Metric Chart 125

Index 126

ACKNOWLEDGMENTS

Many thanks to all the folks who made this book possible. This includes Ron Stokes and Russ Larson, real artists who have put in many years teaching art in the Manitowoc public schools. As I learned how to frame in their classrooms and galleries, I realized how lucky the students of our district are to have such teachers, who guide without forcing and with genuine interest win the hearts and minds of their students.

Mike Cea arranged the materials for this book; no writer could have a better editor. Jim Brewer (and his right-hand assistant, Carolyn) at Freud and Cliff Paddock at CMT Tools provided drawings of their edge-treatment router bits. Jayne Stocker of Fletcher-Terry provided mat-cutting tools and illustrations of them. Mike Watkins of Adjustable Clamp Company provided illustrations of miter boxes and framing clamps. Geoff Brown of Brimarc UK provided the use of, and illustrations for, the Nobex miter box, and he introduced me to many of the better lines of framing tools available in North America. Nancy Elliott of American Art Clay Co. provided photos of Rub'N'Buff and some samples which help to illustrate how easy decorating frames can be. If you have to buy tools and supplies to get started, it pays to buy the best-quality tools you can afford, and these people and their companies supply the best tools. Everyone should have folks as helpful to provide assistance with projects.

My bride of 30 years continues to be supportive of my instructional endeavors, both in the classroom and in print. An occasional framed picture or piece of furniture seems small payment indeed for this sort of support.

I'm sure I'm failing to list some important people without whom the book could not have been done.

While I'm claiming to have had lots of help, where there are errors in the text, they are mine, not those of my contributors.

Russ Larson.

Ron Stokes.

INTRODUCTION

Picture framing—using frames to protect or emphasize artwork—is widely regarded as a complicated process. That's part of the reason why it is often very expensive to have your artwork framed commercially. By using the information in this book and practicing the techniques involved, you will learn the essentials of basic picture framing. This knowledge will permit you to engage in experimentation that will make framing a pleasurable experience for you rather than an expensive nightmare. By the time you have done a few practice frames, you'll realize that you can frame your work at home as well as the professionals do.

Picture framing is a creative, relatively inexpensive craft that can be approached in several ways. The easiest approach is to use prefinished frames from a variety store, for which you only have to prepare the art. Another approach is to carve, shape and finish those frames yourself. You can also create and assemble the frame with simple power tools available in most home workshops. These tools include a radial arm or table saw, a router, some rasps and files, a miter box, hammers, pliers, and paint to finish with. The information in this book, geared for the hobbyist picture-framer, covers all these approaches, so you can choose the one best suited to you.

The essential steps involved in making a picture frame are buying or making moldings, making mats (the protective board around the artwork that separates it from the glass), choosing and cutting the glass, and assembling the artwork in a framed whole. All these steps are examined in the chapters that follow. Other chapters provide an overview of various picture frame designs and projects on which to test your skills. Finally, the glossary on pages 121–124 will clarify any terms with which you are unfamiliar. With the information provided in the following pages, you will soon find yourself engaging in a hobby—and perhaps in a business—that will give you hours of pleasure.

Hugh Foster

SAFETY INSTRUCTIONS

The following instructions will help to minimize operator error in your workshop, thus ensuring a safer working environment:

1. Before using any power tool, read and understand its operations manual. A good manual will describe safe techniques and procedures.

2. Keep the blades sharp and maintain them properly. Dull tools force you to exert extra pressure when you cut. This makes you more likely to slip and get your hands in the way of the cutting edge. A good rule is to sharpen your tool's blade when it starts to feel dull rather than wait until you're sure it is dull.

3. Wear the proper safety equipment when woodworking. Always wear safety glasses or goggles. When using a tool that throws lots of chips, wear a face shield as well. When using a loud tool, wear hearing protection. Wear a dust mask whenever you're sanding or doing operations that produce lots of dust. If there is a dust collector available for the tool, use it every time you switch on the tool.

4. Wear steel-tipped shoes when you are working. Don't wear loose clothing. Roll up your sleeves. If you have long hair, tie it back. Anything loose can be pulled into a blade if it gets caught. Don't wear any type of jewelry.

5. Never attempt to adjust any power tool while it is plugged in or has its battery in place.

6. Do not do any woodworking if you have taken drugs or alcohol. Even over-the-counter and prescription drugs can cause drowsiness and other effects that would make it dangerous to use woodworking tools; so read their labels and follow your doctor's advice.

7. Pay attention to what you are doing. Let your good sense be your guide. Think through each procedure before you do it. If you feel a procedure presents a safety hazard, find an alternative way to accomplish the same result.

Remember, it's important to think about safety on a regular basis. Only your constant vigilance will protect you from injury in the woodworking shop.

Chapter 1

FRAME DESIGN CONSIDERATIONS

What type of picture frame looks good? As a general rule, it seems that a simple, narrow frame is best. Design the frame to complement the art. The simple press-fit European-style frame shown in Illus. 1-1 is an example in which a simple frame works well. While Chapter 5 shows some elaborate styles of moldings—which are the basic outside elements of the frame—generally, relatively narrow, simple frames work better. Home framers can use builders' moldings, framers' moldings, shop-made mold-

ings, and/or combinations of the above, but they shouldn't use so many that the project looks cluttered.

Any artwork done on paper that has some value to the artist should be preserved. Attaching it to a mat—the protective board around the art that separates it from the glazing—protects it. In modern framing, double mats are almost always used. The practice is so common that a single-matted piece looks out of place unless the mats are very fancy-cut,

Illus. 1-1. This Japanese print is mounted in a European factory-made frame. The artwork can be quickly slipped into and out of the frame, as the shadow on the right side of the frame indicates. Even so, the artwork hasn't moved from its position in the frame even though it has been there for at least two decades.

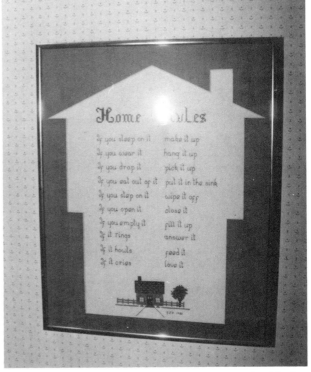

Illus. 1-2. Fancy-cut mats like this one can double the cost of framing. After you get the design onto the mat board, cutting this mat isn't terribly hard, just tedious and fraught with opportunities to err. Mats like these are best left to experienced professionals.

as shown in Illus. 1-2. The commercially cut mat doubled the cost of this framing project, but making a cutout that permits us to view the title, the printmaker's signature, and the print number is easy to do, even in double mats. Chapter 7 describes how to choose and cut mats.

Some authorities suggest that beginners should make the frame first so if the size is off, the mat, glass, etc., can be adjusted to fit. I'm not sure I agree. That's what happened to the print of the Chinese lilies shown in Illus. 1-3. You'll note that the outer mat seems too narrow all the way around the frame, a problem that wouldn't exist had the frame been cut a couple of inches bigger in each direction. Generally, it is better to make the frame too large than too small. After all, a frame that is too large can always be cut smaller, while the reverse cannot be done. Illus. 1-4–1-12 show some other design considerations.

Illus. 1-3. This reproduction of Chinese lilies has a mat so narrow that the whole work looks compressed. I'd like to see another inch of mat added to each edge.

Illus. 1-4. This well-framed print has a reveal cut in it that shows the title, the artist's signature, and the print's number. Most viewers agree that this kind of framing is far handsomer than the framing of a print that leaves a (usually white) border around it so that the signature will show. Contrast this print with the one shown in Illus. 1-11.

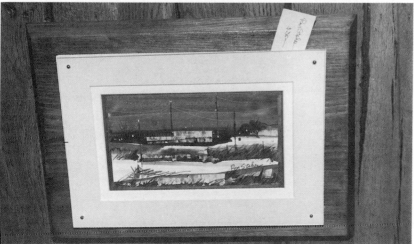

Illus. 1-5. A frame isn't always mitered. Here's a simple frame which shows a matted work set on a plaque, with a sheet of Plexiglas placed over it and four small roundhead screws to hold it in place.

Illus. 1-6. Like the frame shown in 1-5, this one, which is from the author's woodworking shop, does not have mitered corners.

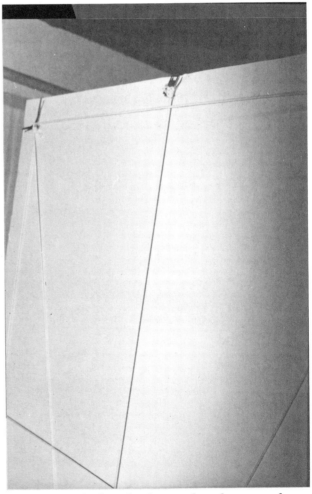

Illus. 1-7 and 1-8. An item like this poster can be mounted and clipped to a sheet of Plexiglas with clips like those shown in Illus. 1-8. I recommend this format only for spaces that are really tight; where this piece hangs, there's simply no room for a frame, not even half an inch!

Illus. 1-8. A look at the clips used on the poster shown in Illus. 1-7.

Illus. 1-9. *This long, slender frame houses a piece of needlework that's nearly as wide as the wall on which it's hung. A needlework project is presented in Chapter 12.*

Illus. 1-11. *A white border has been placed around this print so that the signature may show. Contrast this print with the one shown in Illus. 1-4.*

My friend, architect and artist Malcolm Wells, does most of his work without any visible frames. Instead, he paints on ⅛-inch Masonite which has been bradded and glued to 1-inch-thick × 2-inch-wide lumber that has generally been painted black (Illus. 1-13). He suggests that the Masonite works well and can be handled much more roughly than gilt-edged or glass-filled frames.

Although it is reasonable to expect to make some mistakes as your frames become more complicated, the best way to avoid expensive errors is to plan the project before you begin. Take some time to practice, and when you feel you've mastered the techniques, I'm sure that you'll want to tackle the projects in Chapter 12. These projects represent just a few of the possibilities that present themselves to picture framers.

Illus. 1-10. *Not all frames are cut just at square angles. Note this modern calligraphy's odd-sized pentagonal frame, with the calligraphy extending out into the matting.*

Illus. 1-12. Some artwork can be hung without any frame at all, as this item from the author's workshop shows.

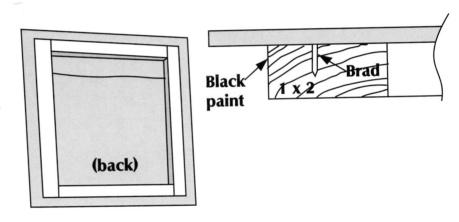

Illus. 1-13. Malcolm Wells's version of the "frameless" painting.

Chapter 2

PICTURE FRAME COMPONENTS

Wooden picture frames consist of seven components: the frame, glass, mat, artwork, backboard, filler, and dust cover (Illus. 2-1). The frame is the component that surrounds the art. There are a few ways to approach frame work. First, you can buy a frame that is ready-made but unfinished and carve some simple designs around the edge. Second, you can buy unfinished picture frame molding at a lumberyard or do-it-yourself store and create your own picture frame. The third approach is to cut your own miters and custom-fit the frame to the art you want to frame.

You are almost certain to want to protect your artwork with glass. You can buy your own glass or cut it. Although it is better to buy the glass if you are only making a few picture frames, knowing how to cut it will prove helpful. Chapter 9 examines glazing techniques.

One way to preserve art in a picture frame is to mount or attach it to a backboard or support. The mat is the decorative and protective board around the art that separates it from the glazing. Both the art and the mat are attached to the matting board.

Filler board, as shown in Illus. 2-1, may be used if the glass, mat board, artwork, and mounting board are thinner than the space provided by the rabbet or channel in the frame. If you're using metal-frame moldings, you will not likely ever need filler to take up space. The ⅛-inch-thick foam-core board filler shown in Illus. 2-1 provides rigidity that takes the place of the dust cover on a frame with wooden molding. If space is important in your metal frame, it is possible to mount your artwork directly to this foam-core filler. A variety of materials, most notably corrugated cardboard, can be used as filler in frames where the rabbet or channel in the frame is too large.

Dust covers are traditionally applied to the backs of artwork framed in wood moldings. The old way of applying the dust cover was to glue paper in place

Illus. 2-1. The components of a picture frame consist of the frame, glass, mat, artwork, backboard, filler, and dust cover. The dust cover is not shown here.

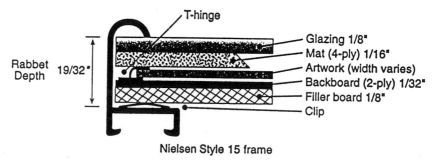

Rabbet Depth   19/32"

T-hinge
Glazing 1/8"
Mat (4-ply) 1/16"
Artwork (width varies)
Backboard (2-ply) 1/32"
Filler board 1/8"
Clip

Nielsen Style 15 frame

over the back of the frame and then sand it flush on all sides, but it is more likely to be applied today with double-sided tape dispensed from an automatic tape gun.

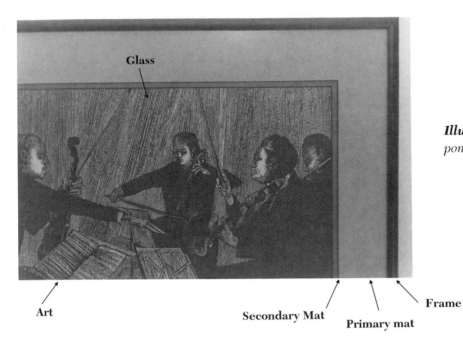

Illus. 2-2. Note the different components of this picture frame.

Glass

Art

Secondary Mat

Primary mat

Frame

Chapter 3

PICTURE-FRAMING TOOLS

Picture framing is a craft that demands little equipment. Assuming that you are buying the frame stock, the major tools and equipment include miter-cutting tools if you want to cut miters on stock, mat-cutting tools, framing clamps, and miscellaneous workshop equipment. All tools and equipment with the exception of mat-cutting tools are examined in this chapter. Mat-cutting tools are described in Chapter 8.

Miter-cutting Tools

If you decide to cut your own miters on stock, you will need miter-cutting tools. Both hand and motorized motor saws are available (Illus. 3-1). The least-expensive handsaw will cost a few dollars, and the most expensive motorized version I'm aware of has a list price of well over a thousand dollars.

Spare parts list

Description	D. Saw arm with	H. Upright short	L. Support tube
A. Table	rivet	I. Length stop	M. Tension rod
B. Pivoted arm	E. Saw arm at	complete	complete
complete less	handle with rivet	J. Material clamp	N. Handle with
uprights	F. Foot	complete	screws
C. Locking catch	G. Upright long	K. Blade guide	O. Center bolt
complete		complete	

Illus. 3-1. The parts shown here for the Nobex Proman hand miter saw are typical of the parts found on other hand miter saws.

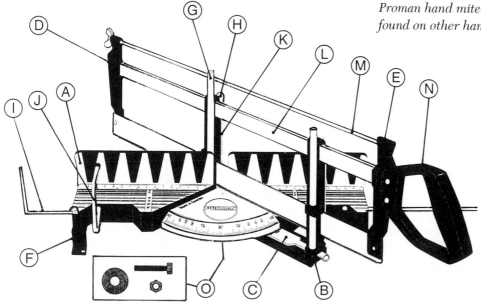

The quality of these saws is relative to their cost. The very inexpensive wooden miter boxes are not worth the money; after you have cut approximately half a dozen lengths of molding, the cut will no longer be square. The metal miter boxes from Jorgensen and Nobex are better values. The Jorgensen Clamp & Saw tool (Illus. 3-2) is said to produce professional-quality left and right 45- and 90-degree miters. It has two material clamps, adjustable saw roller guides, and countersunk mounting holes. The die-cast aluminum base has a durable enamel finish. The tool is useful for permanent- or vise-mounted operation. To use this miter box, you must provide your own saw.

Illus. 3-2. *The Jorgensen #63010 Clamp & Saw tool includes material clamps for securing work and two countersunk mounting holes for stable mounting. Constructed of die-cast aluminum, it produces accurate fixed 45- or 90-degree angles. Also included are adjustable saw roller guides to accept backsaws of varying thickness. The clamps can secure material up to 4 inches wide and 1¾ inches high.*

Jorgensen also has a six-angle box (Illus. 3-3), which is said to be accurately designed for the serious home-project enthusiast. It offers easy, rapid adjustment to fixed settings (left and right) for 90-, 60-, 45-, 30-, 22.5-, and 15-degree cutting angles. It features a die-cast saw guide, depth- and thickness-cutting adjustments, mounting slots, a 14-inch base length, and a back fence that is 3 inches high.

Illus. 3-3. *The Jorgensen #63145 six-angle miter box is designed for the serious home-project enthusiast. Fixed right and left settings for 90-, 60-, 45-, 30-, 22.5-, and 15-degree angles can be easily and quickly adjusted. The tool's table is 14 inches long × 3½ inches wide.*

Jorgensen's #64016 Professional miter saw is a precision-crafted, quality saw for the accurate cutting of miters (Illus. 3-4). It is used by professionals for cabinetry, framing, moldings, and other types of home or professional carpentry. The automatic quick-lock settings and the adjusting lever provide for common and variable angle-cutting. The saw has a depth-of-cut regulator, an adjustable length stop, and a material clamp. This is the least expensive miter box that includes a saw. Its solid one-piece aluminum base and back-fence construction ensure built-in accuracy, and an aluminum finish ensures a long life.

Jorgensen's #64020 Professional compound miter saw is a professional-quality miter saw for the precise cutting of simple and compound miters and bevels (Illus. 3-5). It's ideal for cabinetry, framing, moldings, paneling, and other types of home or professional carpentry. The automatic quick-lock settings and the adjusting lever provide for common, variable, and compound-angle cutting. The saw features a depth-of-cut regulator, an adjustable length

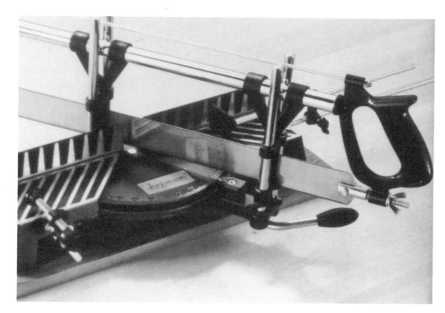

Illus. 3-4. The Jorgensen #64016 Professional miter saw has a 14-TPI (teeth per inch) blade for general-purpose cutting. Its table is 15½ inches long × 3 inches wide. Its back fence is 1½ inches high, and its maximum cutting height is 4¼ inches.

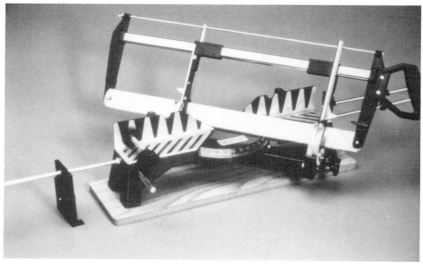

Illus. 3-5. The Jorgensen #64020 Professional compound miter saw produces precise simple and compound miters and bevels. It is ideal for cabinetry, framing, moldings, panelings, and other types of home or professional carpentry. Quick-lock settings and an adjusting lever provide for common, variable, and compound angle cutting. Solid one-piece aluminum construction ensures a built-in accuracy. Other features include a depth regulator, an adjustable length stop, and work-support extensions.

stop, a work-support extension, and a vertical/horizontal material clamp. Its one-piece aluminum base and back-fence construction ensure a built-in accuracy. It's my belief that this saw, which costs approximately $100, will save you enough time and money over the long run to justify its extra expense.

A similar line of saws is available from the Swedish company Nobex. The Nobex Champion 180 miter saw (Illus. 3-6) features a 25-inch-long high-tension blade for even straighter cuts, automatic saw suspension for easy positioning of the workpiece, stepless locking at any angle, preset locking for 4-, 5-, 6-, 8-, and 12-sided frames, and 90-degree cuts. The Champion's table has a variety of slots that

ensure easy cutting of compound miters. Two clamps hold the workpiece firmly, ensuring good results. A "parallel parking" feature is very useful when storing and transporting the tool. This feature allows the blade to be stored parallel to the tool rather than perpendicular to it.

In my shop, I sampled the Nobex Proman miter saw (Illus. 3-7), another advanced compound-miter saw. It has a 22-inch-long blade, a 4-inch depth of cut, and a 3-inch-wide, 14-inch-long table. The assembly time for this saw was under five minutes, and was extremely easy. It would be a good idea to fasten the saw, after assembly, to a board so you can clamp the saw to your bench during use. In use, the com-

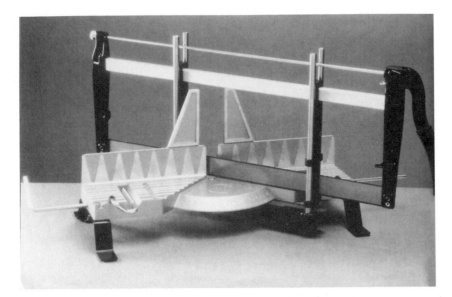

Illus. 3-6. The Nobex 180 Champion miter saw may be suitable for someone who is more than an occasional framer.

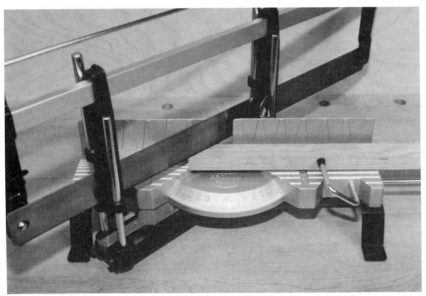

Illus. 3-7. The Nobex Proman miter saw is an excellent saw for those who want to use a handsaw when making picture frames. Its extra-fine blade provides a very smooth cut.

fortable new-style blade and handle proved to be smooth-cutting. There are stops for angles that are set for cutting objects with 4, 5, 6, 8, or 12 sides. There is also a dead-square mechanism that looks like one that will definitely stay square. Of course, one could stop and lock in virtually *any* angle with the saw. Handy and fairly light-duty clamps and end stops make it easy to accurately match cuts. The grooves in the bed of the miter box are used to set pieces which are to be cut for compound miters, at angles set out at 5-degree increments from 20 degrees through 55 degrees (Illus. 3-8). The manufacturer cautions us to saw with a light touch for smoothest results—but that should be so basic as to almost go without saying.

Nobex suggests that the workpiece be set on the table so that the saw teeth will cut into the side that will remain visible. This will ensure a perfect joint. Right-handed people should feed the work from left to right. Clamp the workpiece to the table and ensure that it lies firmly against the vertical way and the horizontal surface. When sawing, press it down with your left-hand thumb (if you're right-handed), as shown in Illus. 3-9. Measure carefully, using a tape measure that covers the whole length of the workpiece. These instructions will work for any

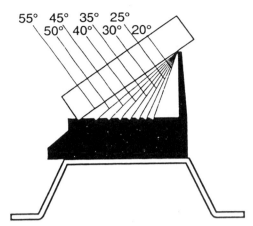

Illus. 3-8. *Cut compound miters at the angles shown by placing the work in the grooves or slots in the table of the Nobex Proman's horizontal surface and flat against the vertical wall.*

Illus. 3-10. *The Lion Miter-Trimmer, shown here without any accessories.*

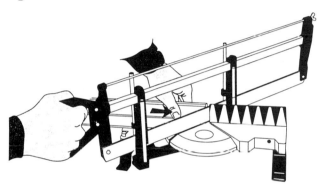

Illus. 3-9. *Right-handed people should feed the work-piece from left to right, clamping it to the table and ensuring that it lies firm against the vertical wall and horizontal surface. When sawing, press it down with your left thumb if you're right-handed.*

brand or type of hand miter saw, but I believe the Proman or the Champion would be my choice.

Still, it's not necessary to have a manual saw. In the past, I most often used the miter gauge on my table saw to cut 45-degree lengths approximately where I wanted them, and then refined the cut precisely to length with the Lion Miter-Trimmer (Illus. 3-10), a guillotine-action tool made by the Poot-atuck Corporation, P.O. Box 24, Windsor, Vermont 05089. The accuracy the Lion Miter-Trimmer affords is unmatched by a standard miter box, and the miter box cannot be used to cut simple and compound miters, bevels, rounds, square ends, and chamfers as can the Lion Trimmer. The Lion Trim-

mer has a lever-(rather than gravity-) operated cutting action. Its infeed table can be adjusted from somewhere just outside of square (90 degrees) to somewhere *just* inside of 45 degrees. This guillotine action produces a razor-smooth cut rather than the sawn cut given by the standard miter box (Illus. 3-11). Part of the reason for the tool's great accuracy is that it is made of a single massive casting, which is 24 pounds of carefully machined cast iron. Its knives are honed razor-sharp, ready for use. Its 90- and 45-

Illus. 3-11. *One chop with the Lion Miter-Trimmer results in clean shavings like this.*

degree positive stops, located on both cutting areas, have been carefully set at the factory. There are Taiwanese imports that look identical for about half the price, but my general experience is that these copies don't work nearly as well.

When using the Lion Miter-Trimmer, cut the piece to length at roughly whatever angle you want, and then trim it, say 1/64 inch or less at a time, until its fit is perfect. Always clamp the Lion Trimmer in place when using it (Illus. 3-12). Holding it by hand could be dangerous. In a framing or other shop where the tool is in constant use, it might be advisable to screw or bolt the tool to the table to keep it from moving. This makes operating the trimmer accurately much easier, although if you use it as a trimmer rather than as a chopper the lever action is quite easy even without the clamping.

Illus. 3-12. Always clamp the Lion Miter-Trimmer in place when using it.

A pair of fairly recent attachments make the tool even more useful. The first is a measuring attachment (Illus. 3-13) that extends the cutting channels by nearly two-and-a-half feet. With some judicious use of spring clamps, one can cut precise lengths repeatedly. This measuring attachment now features a stop block that can be screwed into place, and one can use it to "walk" the piece being cut into the cutter head to produce cuts micrometer-like in precision. Another new accessory is the top trimmer (Illus. 3-14), which is used to cut compound miters.

A fairly recent addition to my shop is the Makita LS1211 compound-miter-cutting slide-action miter box (Illus. 3-15 and 3-16). These power miter boxes are essentially portable circular saws mounted on a stand that permits the saw to pivot vertically and swing laterally. As such, they are good for miter-cutting and for cutting compound angles in rather narrow stock, but in a small workshop where space is limited, there may not be room for them. You may make an exception with the Makita miter box. It has a 10-inch, 50-tooth thin-kerf blade and is a powerful and compact, although relatively expensive, bench-top tool that's good for a variety of crosscutting tasks, including quite specifically mi-

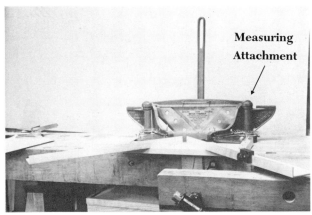

Illus. 3-13. The Lion Miter-Trimmer shown here with the measuring attachment.

Illus. 3-14. The Lion Miter-Trimmer with the top trimmer in action.

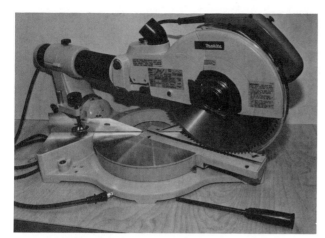

Illus. 3-15. The Makita LS1211 compound-miter-cutting slide-action miter box.

Illus. 3-16. The underside of the Makita saw reveals carefully ribbed castings which help to ensure a long life.

tering and beveling. It can be quickly and accurately set for a variety of miter and bevel cuts and then reliably returned to square.

The Makita LS1211 compound-miter-cutting miter box slides on a single rail like a radial arm saw and pivots downward like a power miter box. To use it, pull the carriage out, pivot the blade into the work, and then push through the cut to prevent the blade from grabbing and to ensure that it is out of the way when you're done. A brake stops the blade virtually instantly when you release the trigger. This is one of the few power miter boxes I've encountered that cuts smoothly enough for picture-framing. And it can cut through an arc of up through

120 degrees. Because the *turntable* shifts to 60 degrees either side of square and the blade tilts to 45 degrees either side of square, there appears to be no imaginable angle that cannot be cut. The telescoping action seems to permit a 12¼-inch maximum width of cut.

There are accurate detent stops at 15, 22½, 30, and 45 degrees. The detents pop firmly in place, so repeat cuts can be easily set. Further, I suspect the cutoff capacity at any degree has just been effectively doubled by the accuracy with which the settings are made: what's to prevent you from cutting 12 inches of stock at 0 degrees and then flipping the board 180 degrees and cutting 12 inches more, netting you a 24-inch crosscut? The saw is, in fact, that accurate. While the widths shrink considerably as the angle increases (to roughly 7¾ inches at 45 degrees and 5½ inches at 60 degrees), the same principle applies: flip the board, and effectively double the width. If you're doing this double-width cutting on a bevel, the bi-directional tilt of the blade makes the process even easier. An excellent clamp-in, built-in clamping system helps to ensure precision.

When I first cut with the Makita LS1211 compound-miter-cutting saw, I realized that fastening it to a bench was a very good idea. The saw started up with such a burst of power that, had it been a router, it probably would have propelled itself right out of my hand. I didn't make the first cut; instead, I stopped and clamped the saw to the bench. I dropped my plans to build a storage space for the tool, for I found that excellent roller bases are available for this saw.

The short fence on either side of the blade is enough for cutting short lengths of stock, but use the extension rails for longer cuts. The standard rails supplied with the saw will set up for repetitive work that is about 18 inches long. A work clamp is standard; a second clamp would be an excellent optional purchase, and the optional cross vise would be another wise investment.

The adjustable plastic kerf plate comes open quite wide. When cutting fine stock, you should set this kerf much narrower. You should also have a replacement set of plates on hand, or make a replacement set from thin wood.

When using the dust bag, you'll find that a fair

amount of sawdust flies around, but the dust bag attaches to an opening that's exactly the size of a standard shop-vacuum hose (Illus. 3-17). The Makita LS1211 saw will accept a hose attachment that permits you to connect the tool to a shop vacuum or another dust-extraction system (Illus. 3-18). If you plan to use it primarily in your shop, buy the dust hose and use it regularly. Also, although this powerful tool runs smoothly, it produces 90–102 decibels of noise, so operators (and other people who work in close proximity) should wear hearing protection (Illus. 3-19).

This tool has other features that are superior to those of most miter boxes, even if you do not con-

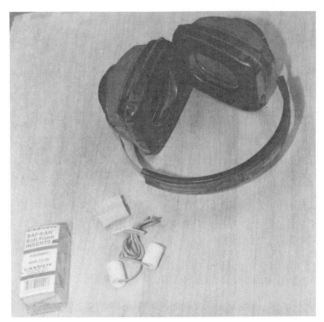

Illus. 3-19. Wear some type of hearing protection when using a miter saw or other noisy tool.

sider its sliding feature. For instance, a spindle lock permits easy blade changing with *one* wrench. Its ingenious see-through blade guard rides a multi-pivot, and it does exactly what it's supposed to do without ever being in the way.

This tool cuts on the push stroke, all but eliminating any kind of kickback. (Kickback occurs when the stock is trapped between the blade and a stationary object such as a fence or guard and is flung back at the operator.) Other safety features include an electric brake and a removable lock-off button.

While I'm partial to this Makita miter box, you may find a 10-inch miter box like the Makita LS1011 or one of its competitors to be perfectly satisfactory. Furthermore, you may find, as you decide to work mostly with commercial frame molding, that most vendors now sell molding in pairs, cut to "whole inch" lengths, so that no sawing at all is required. Before you spend a lot of money on your miter-cutting tools, make sure of exactly what you need.

Safety Instructions for Using Miter Boxes and Saws

Miter saws, like all power tools, should be used carefully. Observe the following safety instructions when using miter saws:

Illus. 3-17. When using a miter box, use a dust bag and wear hearing protection.

Illus. 3-18. A shop-vacuum hose is attached to the miter saw.

1. Read the owner's manual supplied with the saw and review its safety precautions.

2. Use hearing protectors and protective glasses or goggles.

3. Make all adjustments and blade changes with the power disconnected.

4. Make sure that the saw is mounted securely to a work surface or bench. It must remain stable during use.

5. Properly adjust and lock the fences, stops, and clamps before cutting. Use all safety features on the machine.

6. Make sure the stock is clamped securely to the table and fence before making any cuts.

7. Keep your hands clear of the blade's path when using any mitering machine.

8. Allow the blade to come up to full speed before starting the cut. Keep the cord clear of the blade's path.

9. Do not force the saw.

10. Never attempt to hold pieces that are less than 12 inches long with your hands. Use the clamps that come with the miter saw.

Basic Maintenance Techniques

It is important that you maintain your miter saw, vise, and any other tool you have in your workshop regularly. Basic maintenance of a miter saw would include simple steps like keeping the cutters sharp, and keeping glue and sawdust out of the machine because they will prevent wood that is being cut from sitting "square" to the cutter. As you remove the glue, give your saw a shot of WD40 oil to keep it ready for use (Illus. 3-20). If you keep your framing tools sharp, clean, and lubricated, they will serve you better and longer.

Framing Clamps

Because picture framing requires assembly of four (or more)-sided objects that have mitered joints at every corner, more than just a basic bar clamp is needed to hold them together (Illus. 3-21). Each of the clamps discussed here is, in its respective price range, a good value. How much you are willing to spend on your framing clamp may govern your

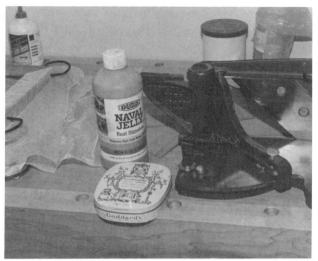

Illus. 3-20. *An occasional bit of clean-up with rust dissolver and a good coat of wax will help to ensure that your tools really do last a lifetime.*

choice more than its function. Of course, if you are working "by the job," the clamp that saves you some time in the long run may be worth more than the one that saves you a few dollars immediately. While string, wire, and band clamps can be used for carcass-framing applications as well, the information in this section concentrates on the clamps best suited for picture framing.

Woodcraft Supply has generally the best selection of clamps of any of the mail-order vendors. Woodcraft's #07S51 Four-Corner Framing Clamp consists of four corners, four connectors, four finger nuts, and eight pieces of ¼-inch-diameter × 24-inch-long threaded rod (Illus. 3-22). The threaded rods go through one side of the corner brackets, and screw into the other side. They can be joined together for multiple lengths.

In theory, threaded rods are easier to work with than clamps with wire, cord, or bands. In practice, using these framing clamps takes a lot of experimentation. When I clamped my first frame with all eight pieces of threaded rod, it got so cumbersome that some of the rods bent. I'll probably replace the bent pieces with 36-inch-long sections of threaded rod. This will reduce the problems to a minimum, at least when I'm clamping frames in the 20-inch-wide × 32-inch-long size range. Given a production run of any size frame, this would be the clamp that I'd want to

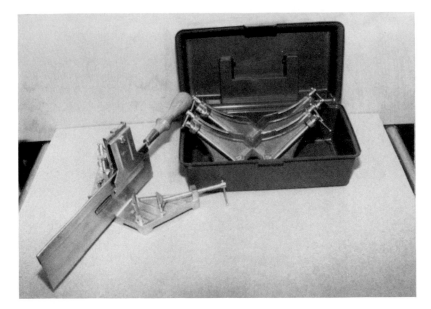

Illus. 3-21. The miter guide and clamps contained in this tool chest are about the amount needed for picture framing.

Illus. 3-22. The Woodcraft #07S51 clamp consists of threaded rod with nuts and corners.

(Illus. 3-24) is stronger than the cord clamp and clamps more quickly and more tightly. It has two cam-tightened belt positions, and a tightening screw to be used only after the web is pulled as tight as possible and cam-locked in place. If it is important that your framing clamp be light, easy to use, and equipped with a powerful clamping action, this may be the best choice.

The Jiffy clamp (Illus. 3-25 and 3-26) is a metal clamp with adapters for curved or molded surfaces. Its ³⁄₁₆-inch-thick wire is drawn tight with a standard turnbuckle. The only real drawbacks to this older

use, for it holds its shape far better than any other clamp.

The Wolfcraft #3417 cord clamp has right-angle corners connected by heavy string (Illus. 3-23). It has a two-meter-long piece of spring-loaded heavy string, four square corners, and a cam-action stopper. I really like the action of the cam-clamp here. Unfortunately, the string has so much "flex" in it that the clamp cannot be made to stay very tight. Since miter joints are only as good as they're *cut*, not clamped, maybe this relatively loose fit isn't a problem.

The more expensive Wolfcraft #3416 belt clamp

Illus. 3-23. The Wolfcraft #3417 cord clamp has a two-meter-long piece of spring-loaded heavy string, four square corners, and a cam-action stopper.

clamp are that it is possible to scratch a couple of frames while tightening the turnbuckle, and that the wire tends to become somewhat distorted, especially after it has been excessively tightened a few times. On the other hand, this clamp will span a 25-foot perimeter. It has been the old standby framing clamp in my shop for the past couple of decades,

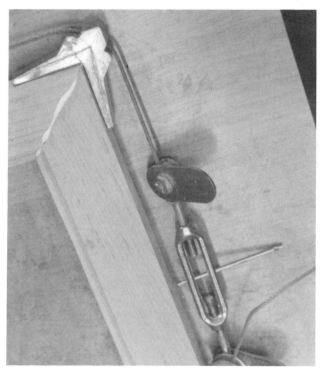

Illus. 3-26. *After you draw the Jiffy clamp tight by hand, you bring it to working tension with the turnbuckle. For decades, this clamp has been one of the most used clamps in my shop.*

Illus. 3-24. *The Wolfcraft #3416 belt clamp is stronger than the cord clamp. It has two cam-tightened belt positions and a tightening screw that is used only after the four-meter-long web is pulled as tight as possible and cam-locked in place.*

and I believe that it is as strong or stronger than the Woodcraft clamps.

Another clamp that should be mentioned is the Hirsch Self-Square clamp (Illus. 3-27). This clamp is made of aluminum and plastic, and is very light. It is quick and easy to use. Many woodworking publications offer shop-made variations of this clamp.

The Wolfcraft #3415 mobile clamps (Illus. 3-28) are corner clamps with quick-adjust screws, well-cushioned pads, and a saw-through slot for joint repair. These aluminum clamps, referred to in some catalogues as rapid action miter vises, are very well made, featuring steel liners or the option of replacing the steel with softer liners if you prefer, and push-button screw releases for the rapid assembly, nailing, and gluing of many kinds of workpiece. I wish every clamp I owned that had a screw in it had this quick-adjust feature. Several of these clamps would be useful for carcass assembly, mounting interior shelves, etc. Unfortunately, having several would be expensive.

The Swanson Picture Framing Cut 'n' Clamp set

Illus. 3-25. *The Jiffy clamp is a metal clamp that has a ³⁄₁₆-inch-thick wire that is drawn tight with a standard turnbuckle.*

Illus. 3-27. *Because the Hirsch Self-Square clamp is made of aluminum and plastic, it is very light. It is also quick and easy to use.*

Illus. 3-28. *Wolfcraft's #3415 mobile clamps are corner clamps that are sold singly. Since you would need four for picture framing, using these clamps can be an expensive proposition. On the other hand, if you join miter-framed furniture assemblies, they could prove valuable. I'd hate to be without a set of these clamps in my general woodworking shop, but I seldom use them for picture framing.*

(Illus. 3-29) provides four miter clamps which are well fitted in a small toolbox that is 11½ inches long, 6 inches wide, and 5¼ inches high. It uses any type of miter saw; my old Sears dovetail saw is a virtually perfect match for this accurate clamping set.

The Ulmia Spring Miter Clamp Set (Illus. 3-30)

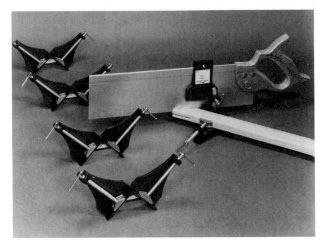

Illus. 3-29. *The Swanson Picture Framing Cut'n' Clamp set consists of four clamps and a mitering tool. The mitering tool accurately guides your saw for corner cuts, and corner clamps hold the pieces securely for fastening. All the parts are made of strong, die-cast aluminum alloy. The saw is not part of the kit.*

is an expensive but handy quick-framing clamp set. The spread springs may leave small marks, but after you have had a bit of practice choosing the right-size springs for the miter you are working on, the springs will touch the frame only where you're likely to drill for a brad. If one made lots of frames, as in a professional framing shop, the cost of this would be warranted, particularly if one used many pieces of large, heavy frame stock. These clamps grab the right-size

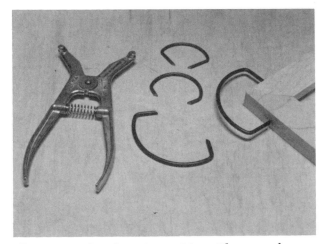

Illus. 3-30. *The Ulmia Spring Miter Clamp set does an admirable job of joining 45-degree miters in a variety of sizes.*

frame very tightly and hold it well. The six sizes of available clamps will handle frame stock that ranges in width from ⅜ through 3½ inches. I can think of only one single complaint about the Spring Miter Clamp Set: the spring clamps should come in multiples of four because four are used to clamp a picture frame; a package of 8 or 12 clamps seems more useful than one with 10. These Ulmia spring clamps are far handier for clamping right-angle frames than any of the clamps previously mentioned, so, despite their rather high cost, they are worthy of your consideration.

The Adjustable Clamp Company sells a Pivoting Jaw clamp (Illus. 3-31). This pivot clamp takes all my strength to operate. If your hands are even a bit smaller than mine or you are even slightly weaker, you'll need two hands to operate it. Carelessly used, this clamp will scar the wood, but it is very effective. Its jaw will open to three inches, and the pivoting jaw pads each have ten small, sharp teeth. A set of four would be required for most framing jobs, which would put this in the more expensive range of framing clamps.

the framing clamp that's most regularly used in my shop these days.

The Proman Framing Clamp Set (Illus. 3-35) is an inexpensive 4-, 5-, 6-, 7-, and 8-sided light-duty clamping kit. Approximately 7 feet of ⅛-inch-thick cord feeds through the loops, and then locks into a series of serrations. This is a very light-duty clamp, so it's important to cut the miters accurately.

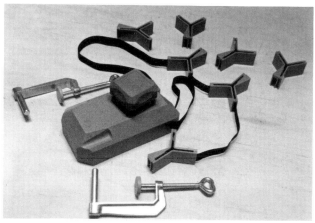

Illus. 3-32. *The components of the Bessey #PA21 band clamp.*

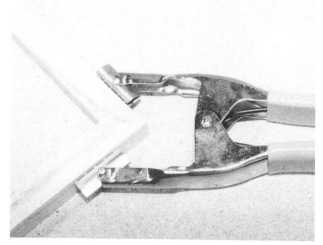

Illus. 3-31. *The Pivoting Jaw clamp holding the pieces of a picture frame together.*

All the clamps discussed so far work best with right angles. The Bessy #PA21 band clamp (Illus. 3-32–3-34) is set up for right-angle frames *and* for clamping hexagonal and octagonal frames, and it can be used as a band clamp for other shapes. This is

Illus. 3-33. *The Bessey band clamp being used to square the corners of a picture frame.*

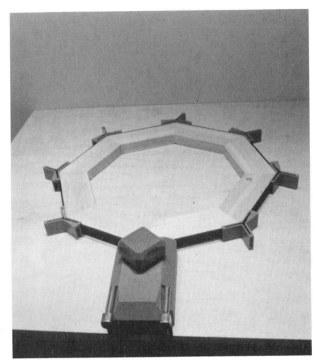

Illus. 3-34. The Bessey clamp is my favorite tool for clamping hexagonal (six-sided) and octagonal (eight-sided) frames. It's set up for these shapes as well as for right-angle frames, and it can be used as a band clamp for other shapes.

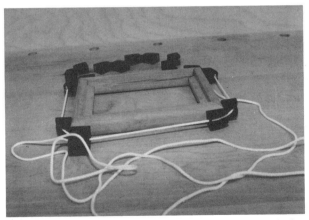

Illus. 3-35. The Proman Framing Clamp set is a light-duty set, run by pulling a length of moderately heavy string through a plastic squeeze clamp.

The preceding information and illustrations will give you some idea of how clamps work, but the best approach is to try out the clamps that look the most interesting to you.

Miscellaneous Framing Tools

Besides those just described and mat-cutting tools, which are described in Chapter 8, a picture framer needs just a few other workshop tools and aids. They are examined below:

1. *Glue.* Polyester glue is especially good for picture framing (Illus. 3-36). It is sold under trade names such as Gorilla Glue and Excel. These excellent glues should be applied to only one of the two surfaces being joined—and sparingly to that one. Polyester glues are more likely than the commonly used polyvinyl acetate (PVA) glues to fill small gaps that might remain in miters that are cut less than perfectly. Unlike PVA glues, which dry rock-hard and leave difficult-to-remove stains on hardwoods, polyester glues can be scraped or sanded away neatly and easily.

Illus. 3-36. The new polyester glues such as Excel and Gorilla glues are perfect for framing.

To remove dried glue, use a random orbit sander on the outside of the channels and a chisel on the inside of the channels where the pictures will go. Better yet, apply finish to your frame stock before cutting and assembling the frame. Then wipe up any excess glue while it is still wet. If at all possible, wash off visible chunks of wet glue.

2. *Skew-angle chisel.* A skew-angle chisel is great for cleaning glue from the inside edge of mitered joints (Illus. 3-37).

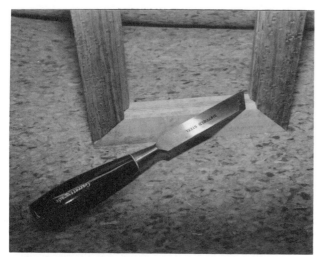

Illus. 3-37. *A skewed chisel like this one is ideal for removing glue squeeze-out.*

3. *Tape gun.* A tape gun is almost essential for matting, mounting, and assembling the frame. United Manufacturer's Supplies provides such a gun made by Cellux (Illus. 3-38). The gun is easy to load. The tape is extremely sticky. There's a large opening in the gun, and a not very well defined cutter. I would store the tool in a Ziplock resealable bag to control dust. This is definitely not a tool to keep in the workshop except during the actual moments of use. If you don't use all the tape, the excess tape can form into gummy balls.

4. *"Bone."* A "bone" (Illus. 3-39) is a tool used to burnish the freshly cut edges of your mats. Burnishing is described in Chapter 8. Once, these bones were made of ivory, but today's version of the tool is made of beef bones.

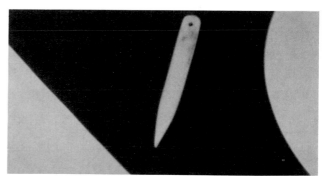

Illus. 3-39. *If you can find an old tool like this, use it to burnish your edge.*

5. *Nail set.* A nail set is used to push the brad deeper than your hammer can reach (Illus. 3-40).

6. *Small drill.* A small drill might be useful for drilling pilot holes for your brads (Illus. 3-40). I find that the 1/16-inch bit from a set of regular "fractional" drills works the same as with larger brads, but that drills numbered from #45 through #60 from the "numbered" set may be preferable for small brads.

7. *Ruler, straightedge, and square* (for measuring 90-degree corners). As with almost any kind of project, these tools are sure to be handy.

8. *Point driver.* Point drivers are used to attach the artwork assemblies to the frames. They drill the brads into the frame. A point driver isn't absolutely necessary; after all, you could force brads into place with a pair of pliers. If you're going to frame only a single piece every few years, that's probably what

Illus. 3-38. *The Cellux tape gun from United Manufacturer's Supplies is shown here open so you can see how simple the threading pattern is. Simply spool the tape off the roll around the big roller, and pull the leader until you can feed the carrier tape into the take-up reel at the right. Then close the side, and you're ready to tape.*

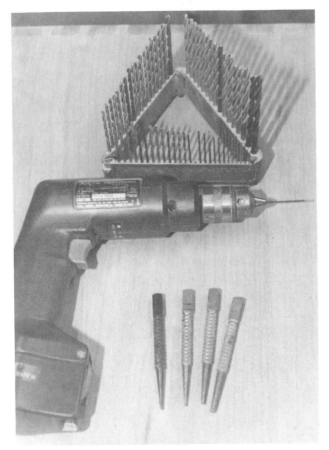

Illus. 3-40. A nail set and drill.

.015 inch thick, and they can be easily bent upward to remove backing material, and then bent back down to hold new material firmly in place. Finally, there is a pneumatic FrameMaster for framers who do lots of frames every day; it uses up to 100 PSI (pounds per square inch) from your compressor, and features a finger-grip trigger and a safety switch to prevent accidental firing.

9. *Utility knife* (Illus. 3-44). This is a tool with a

Illus. 3-41. The Fletcher-Terry Framemate is a handy and affordable tool for inserting framer's points into wooden picture frames up to three inches wide.

you should use, but if you're going to do framing regularly, you should probably invest in some sort of a point driver. The Fletcher-Terry Company appears to own the market, with five models that include the FrameMate (Illus. 3-41), a handy and inexpensive tool for inserting framer's points into wooden picture frames up to 3 inches wide; the FlexiDriver (Illus. 3-42), a versatile and dependable driver which fires wax-free stacked diamond and triangle points; and the FrameMaster, which fires wax-free framer's and glazier's points perfectly flat to the surface for more holding power. When using the FrameMaster, it's easy to load a magazine that holds 100 points and fires them one at a time without double-feeding or jamming; a rear stabilizer extension keeps the FrameMaster upright for quick access. A contoured full-grip trigger and lightweight design lets you fire the points quickly and comfortably. The FlexiMaster (Illus. 3-43) takes the idea of the FrameMaster one step further: its points are

Illus. 3-42. The Fletcher-Terry FlexiDriver is perhaps the most useful of the point drivers for attaching the artwork assembly to the frame. The reason? Its points can be bent back when an error has been made, and then, after the error has been corrected, the points can be bent forward again.

Illus. 3-43. *The Fletcher-Terry FlexiMaster, the latest design in point drivers, fires flexible framer's points which are only .015 inch thick and which can be easily bent upward to remove backing materials, and then bent back down to hold new materials in place. It has a easy-firing, full-grip trigger and a stabilizer extension to keep the tool upright for quick access.*

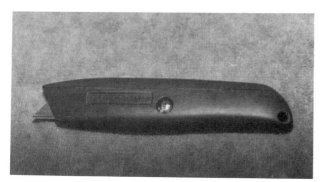

Illus. 3-44. *The Stanley "handy knife."*

replaceable blade that is used to cut the outside of mat board, fabric, and other material.

10. *Screw eyes, wire, and wall hangers.* These are used after you close the assembly to mount the completed framing job onto a wall.

11. *Small-diameter drill bit and awl.* In hard wood, you'll use a small-diameter drill bit after you mark the frame with the awl, but in soft wood you'll be able to drill the holes started for the hooks with just an awl, and then turn the hooks in with the awl working as a lever (Illus. 3-45 and 3-46). Another excellent use for the awl is to use its edge for bur-

nishing any scratched material at the corners of newly assembled frames.

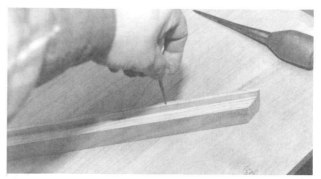

Illus. 3-45. *Using an awl to make the holes for the hooks.*

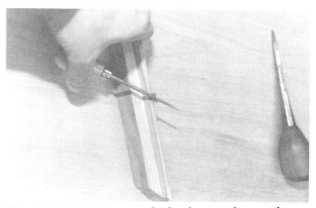

Illus. 3-46. *You can turn the hooks into the wood using an awl as a lever.*

12. *Fine-grit sandpaper.* This will be useful for rounding the edges of rough-cut corners and for sanding excess backing material off completed frames (Illus. 3-47).

Illus. 3-47. *Removing the back of a project with sandpaper doesn't work very well if the back of the frame is curved rather than having square corners, as shown here.*

Chapter 4

DETERMINING THE AMOUNT OF FRAME STOCK NEEDED

Before you can begin to order or cut your frame stock, you have to know how much stock is needed. To determine the amount you need, do the following:

1. Add the four sides of the opening.
2. Factor in the waste wood. To do this, multiply the width of the frame stock by 8.
3. Estimate the loss of space because of the saw kerfs. This can possibly be a whole inch or more around the project.
4. Finally, add the four sides, the waste wood, and the estimated loss of space from the kerfs to arrive at the total amount of frame stock needed.

Let's use the following example to illustrate this (Illus. 4-1). Suppose you want to make a frame 14 inches wide × 22 inches long with 2-inch-wide frame stock. To determine the amount of stock needed, do the following:

1. Add the four sides: 14 + 14 + 22 + 22 = 72.
2. Multiply the width of the frame by 8: 8 × 2 = 16.
3. Add 1 inch to the kerfs.
4. Now, add the three figures you arrived at: 72 + 16 + 1 = 89 inches of frame stock. This means you should buy a straight eight-foot section of molding.

Now, you know how to determine generally the amount of framing stock needed, so it is possible to look at some formulas for cutting specific types of frames. Most objects that are framed are either square or rectangular, so our discussion will mainly cover cutting 45-degree miters. Framing at other angles works exactly the same, if your miter box and framing clamps have the capacity to deal with the

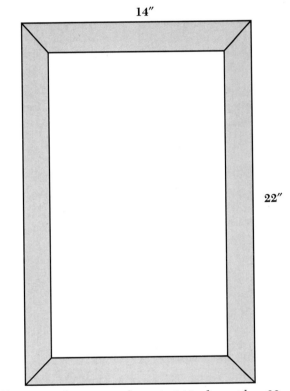

Illus. 4-1. *This picture frame is 14 inches wide × 22 inches long. Do you know how to determine how much stock is needed to make such a picture frame?*

material. Below are the formulas for rectangular, pentagonal, hexagonal, and octagonal frames, which are shown with their angles listed in Illus. 4-3. In the formulas cited, **L** refers to the frame length (maximum length of each side); **S** refers to the side of the picture frame; **W** refers to the width of the

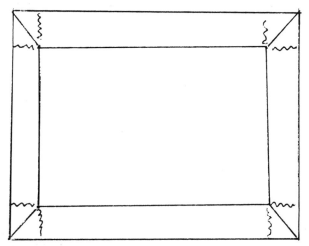

Illus. 4-2. *The broken lines in this drawing represent the overlap of the pieces before they are mitered. The length of the frame pieces is the width of the art plus the width of the non-rabbeted portion of the frame.*

Here is the actual way to calculate the amount of stock needed for frames with various numbers of sides:

For *rectangular frames,* measure the frame width from the rabbet to the outer edge (Illus. 4-4) and add the desired play. Next, multiply this sum by two, and, finally, add the length of the picture side.

For *pentagonal frames,* measure the frame width from the rabbet to the outer edge and add the desired play. Then multiply this sum by 1.453, and, finally, add the length of the picture side.

For *hexagonal frames,* measure the frame width from the rabbet to the outer edge and add the desired play. Then multiply this sum by 1.155, and, finally, add the length of the picture side.

For *octagonal frames,* measure the frame width from the rabbet to the outer edge and add the desired play. Then multiply this sum by .828, and, finally, add the length of the picture side.

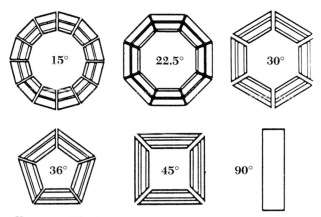

Illus. 4-3. *The frames most commonly used in picture framing, and the angles at which they are cut.*

frame from the rabbet; and **P** refers to the play in the rabbet between the picture and the frame.

Here are the formulas:
Rectangle (4 sides): $L = S + 2 \times P + W$
Pentagon (5 sides): $L = S + 1.453 \times P + W$
Hexagon (6 sides): $L = S + 1.115 \times P + W$
Octagon (8 sides) $L = S + .828 \times P + W$
12 sides (nearly round): $L = S + .536 \times P + W$

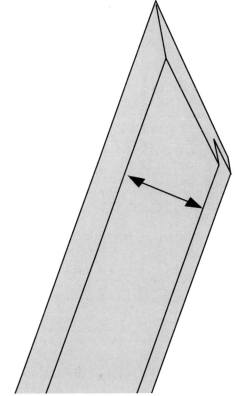

Illus. 4-4. *Measuring the frame width from the rabbet to the outer edge.*

Chapter 5

CHOOSING COMMERCIAL FRAMES AND MOLDINGS

As mentioned previously, a picture-framer can buy a frame and fit the artwork to the frame, buy moldings and make the frame from the moldings, or make the frame stock in his workshop. The easiest way is to buy a frame of the size and design needed for your artwork and fit the artwork to the frame. Choosing commercial moldings and frames is the basis for the information in this chapter.

A recent visit to a small-town framing shop revealed that there were over 600 sample moldings and frames hanging on the wall. How is a person to choose? Ordering precut lengths has advantages, and if you haven't the patience for fancy hole-filling, then you should probably choose simple wooden frames or even metal frames. Simple frames seem to work better than very ornate ones, because they help us focus our attention on the artwork.

There are three basic ways of obtaining commer-

Illus. 5-1. A selection of wood moldings from Graphik Dimensions Ltd.

Illus. 5-2. More moldings from Graphik Dimensions Ltd.

cial frames and moldings. The first is, of course, to pay a visit to your local framing shop. The second is through catalogues offered by companies that sell these products. The third is through garage sales, which are discussed on page 40. As I perused the catalogues on available frames offered by different companies, it occurred to me that several companies are more interested than others in supplying parts to amateur framers and other users of small quantities of molding, and they are supplying moldings that we might not be able to buy in our local art-supply shops. Below I describe several of the more impressive companies.

Graphik Dimensions, Ltd. (2103 Brentwood, North Carolina 27263) has a full-color catalogue that shows hundreds of designs, ranging from very simple to very ornate (Illus. 5-1 and 5-2). It also offers preassembled baroque frames with large raised areas. (Baroque frames appear to be carved, although the "carvings" are often either pressed into the wood or built up on the wood with plaster-like compositions.) In addition to wooden frames, it sells

metal extruded frames in a wide variety of colors and patterns. It also sells a variety of inexpensive framing kits which include everything that you need for a project other than the artwork and the frame.

Tennessee Moulding and Frame, Inc. (1188 Antioch Pike, Nashville, Tennessee 37211), is the source of Illus. 5-3 and 5-4. The company professes to be a wholesale house servicing only professionals, but if you're ordering more than just a few pairs of frame section at once, it would probably be very happy to fill your order. As the illustrations show, it has a very fine selection of frames.

Emperia, Inc. (1075 West Country Road East, St. Paul, Minnesota 55126) sells only moldings, feeling that it can better serve its customers by "limiting" its product to about 400 moldings. Further, a look at its full-color catalogue will show you that its moldings, mostly from Europe, are unlike those shown elsewhere. If you're looking for something different, Emperia, Inc., is the molding source for you.

United Manufacturers Supplies, Inc. (80 Gordon Drive, Syosset, New York 11791, or 1701 Clint

5 This profile features the same graceful rounded face as Profile #15, with just the rabbet depth you need for framing posters, photos and single-matted images.

 11 Clean lines and a slightly eased back face have made #11 a favorite for photography, prints and posters.

 12 The same classic face as #11, but with a deeper channel that allows for multiple matting and other more creative framing techniques.

 15 A graceful profile available in a wide range of finishes and colors. Deep enough to allow creativity of framing applications.

 22 This moulding was designed for use with artwork on stretchers or whenever extra dimension is desired. Utilizes the same clean face as profiles #11 and #12. Ideal for many of the latest contemporary framing techniques.

 25 Profile #25 with a dramatic rounded face and its classic lines are suitable for all types of art. Profile #25 is available in two new, exciting finishes and textures. Profile #25 with a subtle design element for all of today's alternatives.

 33* This profile is suggested to obtain the most effective minimal look in framing. Ideal for posters and photos.

 35 Profile 35, with its classic lines, narrow polished face and exceptional depth, is particularly suitable for stretched canvas, creative presentations, dimensional artwork and shadow boxes.

50 Height and width are balanced in this basic flat top design, allowing for a variety of framing applications. #80 can fit into this channel.

 71 Designed to accommodate stretched canvas pictures, this moulding offers elegance and functionality. An elegant round top available in a wide variety of anodic finishes and white.

 73 The elegance of profile #71† taken one step further with sides that are polished like the face.

 74* A wide classic face and the depth to accommodate stretched canvas art, yet, with a lengthened radius, the effect is one of lightness. Used with Nielsen recessed hanger. Foot permits application of dust cover as with #75, #80, and #90.

 75* A classic half-round profile that showcases any image it surrounds, from posters to prints to photographs. The smooth shape enhances the color and gloss of both the anodized and new Colorwave* painted finishes. The deep rabbet accommodates double mouldings, multiple mats, etc. Used with Nielsen recessed hanger.

 80* The low, wide profile of this moulding is gently rounded toward the back, giving it a bold graphic look. Used with Nielsen recessed hanger. Springs clips not necessary.

 81* Simplistic styling combined with a sophisticated "Florentine" finish gives this profile a very distinctive look that is well suited for a variety of artwork and settings.

 83* With its swept back face and cross-hatched finish, this profile offers an extraordinary combination of style and finish, comparable to costly metal-leaf moulding. Use with the Nielsen recessed hanger.

84 Profile #84 illustrates the flexibility as well as creativity attainable with aluminum moulding. Nielsen #84 possesses a classical look with a very tailored and defined ribbed design.

Illus. 5-3. *Profiles of Nielsen Metal Mouldings, illustrated in the catalogue offered by Tennessee Moulding and Frame. These are very likely the metal moldings you'll prefer. Many of these shapes come in 56 colors, so finding exactly the right frame for your project can probably be done right from this page.*

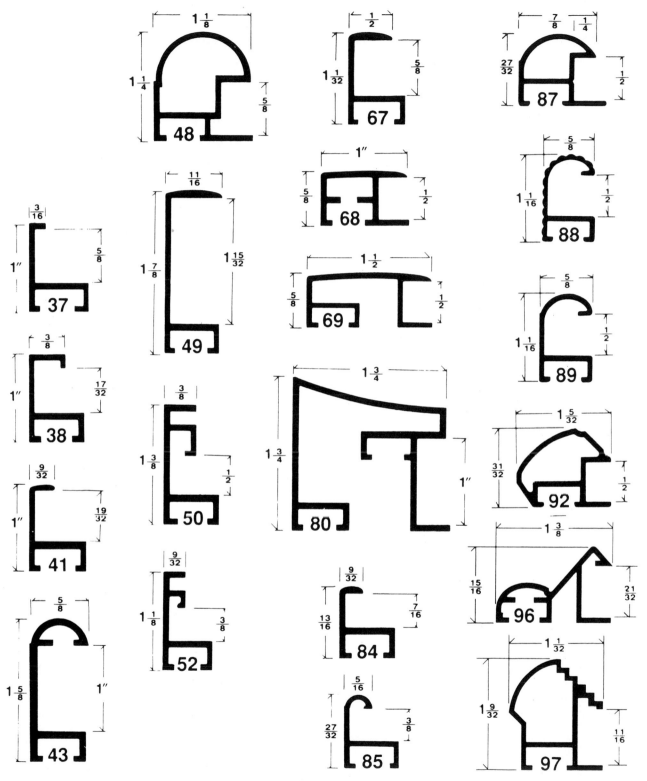

Illus. 5-4. *Profiles of metal moldings from Designer Moulding. In my small-town framing shop, the extrusion shown in the middle of this grouping, which is number 80, sells for $17 per running foot.*

Moore Road, Boca Raton, Florida 33487) has a collection of several catalogues. It offers excellent prices on large and small orders (although its minimum "chop" order is $30) for mat board, moldings, tools, and supplies too numerous to mention, along with excellent, speedy service. ("Chop" molding has been precut or mitered to a specific size.) Its wooden frames are available with or without Taper Lock assembly hardware. (The Taper Lock assembly cuts slots in the back of miter joints and uses inserts that fit into these slots to hold the miters together after glue is applied to the miter. This system permits the framer to avoid using brads to hold frames together.)

Daniel Smith, Inc. (P.O. Box 84268, Seattle, Washington 98124-5568) sells general artist's supplies: oils, acrylics, watercolors, brushes, drawings, pastels, pigments, printmaking equipment, paper, canvas, furniture, and frames. Not only does the company sell good products at reasonable prices, it also offers an instructive catalogue.

The American Frame Corporation (Arrowhead Park, 400 Tomahawk Drive, Maumee, Ohio 43537-1695) bills itself as the "Do-It-Yourself Picture Frame Company." It welcomes orders from amateurs. There is enough information in its catalogue to help most non-framers become framers. This company cuts chops from hundreds of frame patterns to the dimensions of your artwork, and also offers mat board, foam core (a lightweight polystyrene board sandwiched between two smooth papers that is excellent for use as backing), and a variety of other supplies that are sure to be of use to experienced and beginning framers.

One word of advice about ordering catalogues: Don't call for catalogues if you are not interested in buying frames. The catalogues cost a great deal to prepare and mail, and people who aren't shopping are simply driving up prices for those who do buy.

Garage sales are another excellent source of ornate frames. Sometimes these frames will be in need of repair, but one of the best ways to make them look like new is to fill any serious flaws with plaster, sand them smooth, and then refinish with a product like Rub 'n' Buff (American Art Clay Co., Inc., 4717 West 16th Street, Indianapolis, Indiana 46222), which goes on much like "metallic" shoe polish, which it greatly resembles (Illus. 5-5). Chapter 6 describes application techniques for this product. It comes in 18 colors: gold leaf, silver, antique gold, antique white, emerald, sapphire, amethyst, ebony, olive gold, Spanish copper, pearl blue, Grecian gold, jade, Chinese red, pewter, turquoise, European gold, and autumn gold.

Illus. 5-5. *This old frame was brought back to life by judicious application of ebony and gold Run 'n' Buff. Gold highlighting is buffed into the regular finish so that it is not overtly obvious.*

Disassembling a Commercial Picture Frame

Illus. 5-6–5-10 show a commercial picture frame that can be hung or stood up on either its horizontal or vertical plane. Showing this frame disassembled is helpful because it reveals the components of a picture frame. This frame has small adjustable clips that hold the assembly back into the frame. The first step in disassembly is turning each of these adjustable clips 90 degrees so that the back can be removed.

Next, remove the back. As you remove it, you will see that there are two sheets of poor-fitting corrugated cardboard (Illus. 5-8). These filler sheets hold the artwork against either the mat or the glass.

Illus. 5-8. When you remove the back, you see that there are two sheets of poorly fitting corrugated cardboard that hold the picture in place.

Next is the back side of the image being displayed (Illus. 5-9). Finally comes the glass (Illus. 5-10) at the very bottom of the assembly. Even if the glass looks clean, it would probably be a good idea to take it out, wash it, and dry it thoroughly before returning it to the frame.

With the glass removed, we can see that the opening of this 4×6-inch picture frame will display a $3\frac{5}{8} \times 5\frac{3}{8}$-inch photo in a 4×4-inch rabbet that is $\frac{7}{16}$ inch deep and $\frac{3}{16}$ inch wide.

Illus. 5-9. After the cardboard, you arrive at the back side of the image displayed.

Illus. 5-6. A commercial picture frame for a 4-inch-wide × 6-inch-long photograph. The front of it has advertising.

Illus. 5-7. A back view of the picture frame indicates that it can be hung from a wall or stood on a surface either horizontally or vertically. Also note the adjustable clips that hold the back into the frame. It would be nice if these clips were sold by craft supply houses.

Considering that this type of commercial frame can be both inexpensive and attractive, there has to be some special reason to *make* a frame this small. Unless your time has absolutely no value, a frame like this commercial one is really what you want for small items. While the apparently ill-fitting inserts might suggest otherwise, this is a high-quality product—and packing material doesn't really need to fit any better than that.

Illus. 5-10. *The glass is the next item you come across in disassembly. With the glass removed, you will note that the actual opening is 3⅝ inches wide × 5⅝ inches long, and that a ⁷⁄₁₆-inch-deep, ³⁄₁₆-inch-wide rabbet is cut around the 4-inch-wide × 6-inch-long frame.*

Chapter 6

MAKING MOLDINGS

It's possible to frame pictures without ever making your own molding or having to cut the molding. Nevertheless, if you have an even moderately well equipped woodworking shop, you can make handsome moldings that are far less costly than commercial ones, and these moldings may well be uniquely yours. The tools you need are a table saw, a jointer/planer (or a jointer and a planer as separate units), and a router with a router table and a fair selection of bits.

After you have decided on a molding profile, there are a couple of things you ought to do in the shop before you begin. First, get out your hearing protectors, and make sure your dust-collection units are ready to work (Illus. 6-1). Then, with a sharp pencil, draw a pair of straight lines that bring both edges of your table-saw blade all the way down to the front of the table (Illus. 6-2 and 6-3). The more

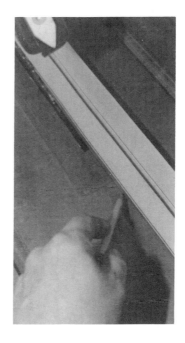

Illus. 6-2. Draw a pair of lines with a sharp pencil that brings both edges of your table-saw blade all the way down to the front of the table.

Illus. 6-1. Be sure to use your dust pick-up system and to wear hearing protection when using power tools.

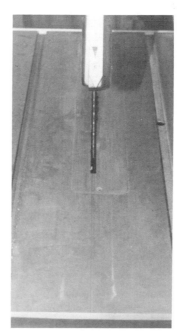

Illus. 6-3. The extended lines.

carefully you do this, the more accurately the lines will help you to gauge your cuts. Secondly, if your miter gauge doesn't have stops, be ready to clamp something in place that will work as a stop (Illus. 6-4); the second piece of molding you cut must be an exact duplicate of the first (Illus. 6-5). However, if you must err, make the piece too long instead of too short.

its length. Don't accept wood with knots, gouges, or other natural or man-made flaws. The visible surface of the frame should be especially good. Check for consistent grain markings if you're going to use a clear finish. Store material carefully to keep it from warp; keep it flat rather than on end.

After you've selected your wood, cut the pieces you'll need off the boards you bought. The boards

Illus. 6-4. *Having a miter gauge like this with a hold-down and stop helps to ensure that the matching sides of the frame are exactly the same.*

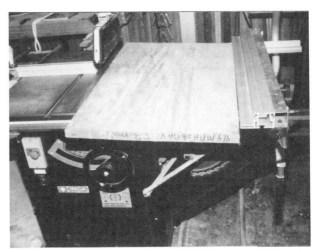

Illus. 6-6. *Cut the stock off the large sheet with a table saw. This prime mahogany will make great-looking frames that won't require much finishing.*

Illus. 6-5. *These matching sides are exactly the same size.*

If you're making your own moldings, use kiln-dried stock, which is less likely to shrink or warp. Check to be sure the material is flat by sighting down

Illus. 6-7. *Cut so the amount you want is away from the fence. There is no point in having to guide a 22-inch-wide board by the 1½ inches that you want from it.*

Illus. 6-8. I cut four strips, enough for two small frames. Notice that they take a sizable piece off this valuable stock.

Illus. 6-9. After you have cut an appropriate number of strips, joint one face and one edge to begin flattening the stock.

you buy won't often be as wide as the piece of mahogany shown in the illustrations, but they'll often be longer. I selected this mahogany because I was sure that it would make great-looking frames that wouldn't require much finishing.

Set your table-saw's fence so that you cut the amount you want on the side opposite the fence; there's no point in having to guide a 22-inch-wide-board by the 1½ inches that you want to cut from it (Illus. 6-6–6-8). Be sure to operate the saw (and all equipment!) with all safety gear in place and functioning, to wear hearing protection around power tools, and to use your dust pick-up system.

After you have cut an appropriate number of strips, joint one face and one edge to begin flattening the stock. Plane the other two sides of each piece. You could joint this stock flat (Illus. 6-9 and 6-10), but the planer makes the stock's surface both flat and parallel.

Select your router bit and mount it on the router table (Illus. 6-11–6-15). After many years of use, the Elu 3304 router, with its small accessory router table, remains a favorite in my shop despite its ability to accept only bits with ¼-inch shanks. If your router table offers any safety or convenience features, you should use them (Illus. 6-16). Use a dust-

collection system. If you don't, you're sure to be breathing too much dust and spending too much clean-up time.

Illus. 6-10. Here one face of the stock is being jointed with a jointer/planer.

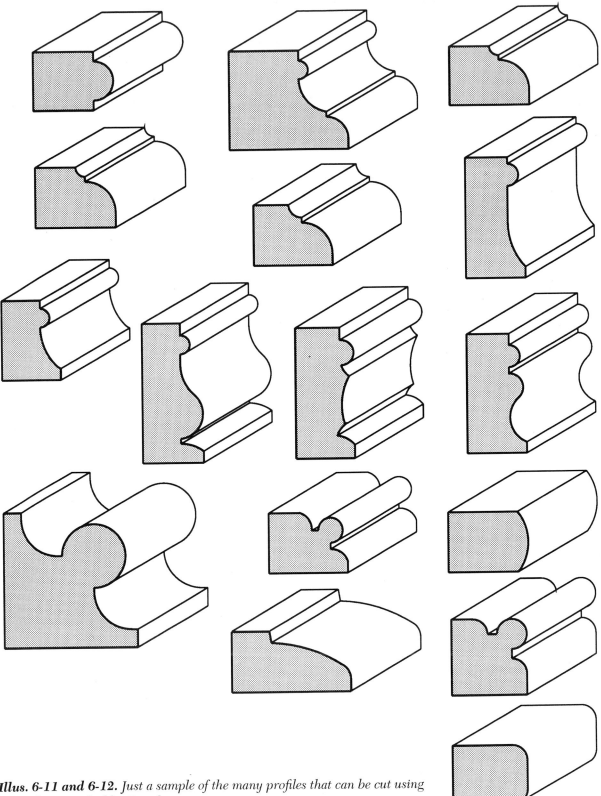

Illus. 6-11 and 6-12. *Just a sample of the many profiles that can be cut using router bits supplied by Freud.*

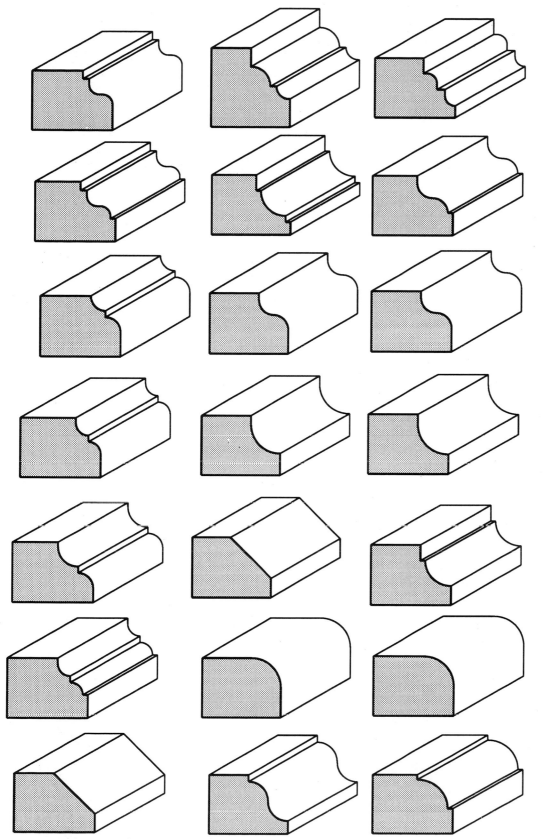

Illus. 6-12.

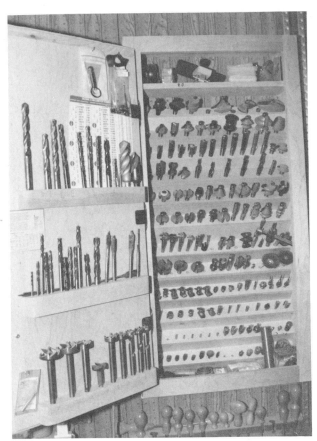

Illus. 6-13. *This collection of router bits is the accumulation of years of woodworking, not a one-time purchase, but if you have such a collection your chance of being able to make some interesting frames is greatly enhanced.*

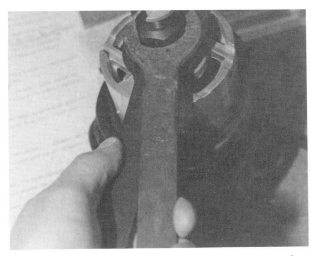

Illus. 6-14. *Select your router bit and mount it in the router table.*

Illus. 6-15. *Be sure to clamp down the router table.*

Illus. 6-16 . *Making the molding cuts.*

For the molding shown in this section, we made two passes with a ⅜-inch quarter-round bit. Illus. 6-17 compares a two-pass molding to the three-pass molding made another day. The two-pass molding is easier to finish on its back, so, for most of us, this one is a better choice. Also, notice that the more slender version is more graceful. This may be the ideal stock for framing most of the simple frames being produced today.

Illus. 6-17. Compare the two-pass molding to the three-pass molding on the left. The two-pass molding is easier to finish on its back.

Illus. 6-19. Measure a rabbet to the outside edge of the table-saw blade.

Feed the stock smoothly to avoid burn marks like the one shown in Illus. 6-18. The minor flaw on this stock will take lots of extra work to remove.

After routing the molding, saw a ¼- × ½-inch rabbet in each piece (Illus. 6-19–6-21). Always set the saw so that the finished dimension is against the fence; this way, wander can be corrected. If you saw with the finished piece on the side of the blade opposite the fence, you risk losing otherwise useful stock. Don't throw away the strips produced while cutting the rabbet; they make great kite sticks (Illus. 6-22)!

Illus. 6-18. Feed the stock smoothly to avoid burn marks like the ones shown here. This minor flaw will take a lot of work to remove.

Illus. 6-20. Sawing a rabbet on a table saw.

Illus. 6-21. Sawing a rabbet on a table saw.

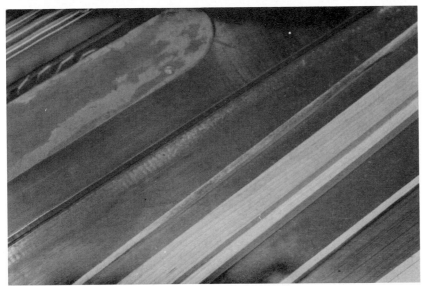

Illus. 6-22. The back side of the molding with the waste stock from the rabbet lying alongside it.

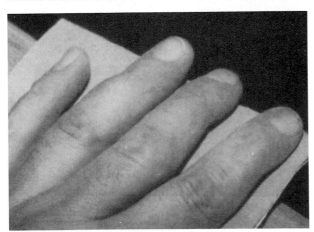

Illus. 6-23. Sand the moldings until you are satisfied they are smooth. I sand solely with or up through 150 grit with regular sandpaper.

Sand the moldings until you're satisfied that they are smooth. I sand either solely with or up through 150 grit with regular sandpaper (Illus. 6-23), and then through 180 or 220 grit with Klingspor sanding sponges (Illus. 6-24). If your molding work has been clean, only minimal sanding should be required. Then wipe the sanding dust off the moldings, and apply two or three spare coats of varnish (Illus. 6-25). I like Bartley's paste varnish, which is wiped on much the same as Danish oil. Three or four coats of the varnish leave an excellent, protective build-up, and the drying time is less than two hours per coat unless the weather is very humid. Most varnishes darken material somewhere between slightly and quite a bit.

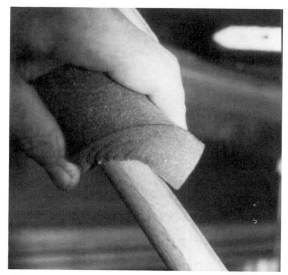

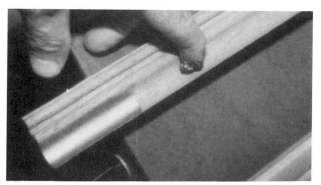

Illus. 6-26–6-28. After the finish dries completely, apply Rub 'n' Buff if desired. This product can be applied with your fingers, as shown here, allowed to dry, as shown in Illus. 6-27, and then buffed off, as shown in Illus. 6-28. You control the amount with a rag. If you apply it to bare wood, it will remain on permanently.

Illus. 6-24. Then sand through 180 or 220 grit with sanding sponges.

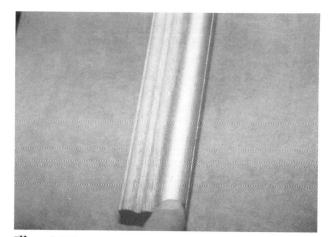

Illus. 6-27.

Illus. 6-25. Wipe off the sanding dust and apply two or three spare coats of varnish. Here I'm using Bartley's paste varnish, which is wiped on much the same as Danish oil. Three or four coats of this varnish leave an excellent protective build-up, and the drying time is less than two hours per coat unless the weather is very humid. Most varnishes darken material from just slightly to quite a bit.

If you're going to use an accent on your finish, it's probably best to apply it at this stage of the operation. One of the easiest products to use is Rub 'n' Buff, a heavy, clay-based, waxlike paint product that

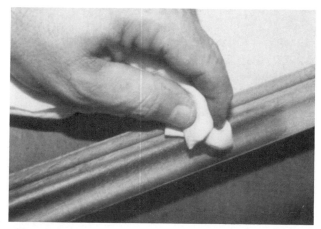

Illus. 6-28.

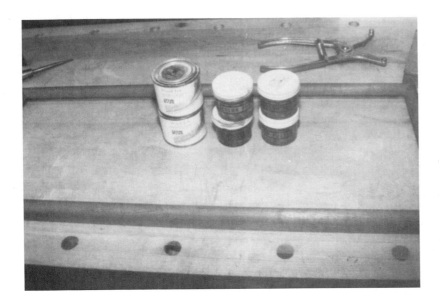

Illus. 6-29. Note the wide variety of different-colored putties used for this fairly simple job. More complex jobs will call for mixed putties, stick shellac, or even a special glazing formula that is made for the particular frame stock.

can be used to "antique" or decorate almost any surface. Simply rub a small amount evenly over the area with your fingers with a gentle rubbing motion (Illus. 6-26), allow it to dry for a while (Illus. 6-27), and then buff it gently with a soft cloth or tissue (Illus. 6-28), much the way shoe polish is buffed on a shoe. By experimenting with the drying time and the amount of wiping, you can have excellent control over the finished appearance of the frame.

Save wood scraps when building a frame so you

can test the finish on them. Spray finish is the safest to use outdoors. I rarely use stain, because stain obscures the natural beauty of the wood. When I want colored frames, I generally use metal. Wear throwaway gloves when adding a finish. Many solvents are absorbed into the body through the skin, so these

Illus. 6-30. Apply the putty with your fingers.

Illus. 6-31. Pushpins placed in the corners will enable you to finish all the surfaces of the frame.

gloves are really an investment in good health. Putty also works well in some cases (Illus. 6-29 and 6-30). Always use pins or brads to support the back side of the workpiece when you're finishing (Illus. 6-31).

Assembly procedures are discussed in Chapter 10.

Making Complex Moldings

More complex moldings are somewhat more difficult to make, but well within the reach of most home

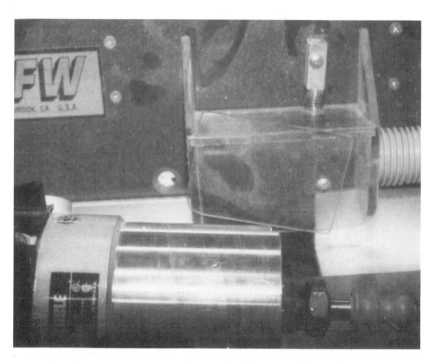

Illus. 6-32. The Porter-Cable #690 router, with a CMT bit, is shown on a CFW router table. This router, bit, and router table are a nearly ideal trio for making moldings. A much narrower opening in the router table would be highly desirable.

Illus. 6-33. This featherboard is a very important safety tool. Even with this featherboard in place, use a heavy-duty push stick. You don't want your hands anywhere near a cutter this big.

workshops. To make these, we must use a larger router table and a router that will hold bigger edge-profile bits, most of which come with ½-inch shanks. The Porter-Cable #690 router has a helical base, which means that the router motor and collet can be easily removed from its base, which, in this case, has been permanently mounted in an CFW tilting router table (Illus. 6-32). The CFW router table is capable of making an almost infinite variety of moldings, even with a fairly limited collection of bits, because the cutting action can be tilted so that moldings may be produced up to 45 degrees off-square. You'll have fun experimenting with a table like this!

For this exercise, I put a CMT #855-901 bit in the router's collet; this bit is just one of the many fine edge-molding bits sold by that company. (In fact, CMT will soon introduce a picture-framing bit set that will contain all the bits a picture framer will need.) The only change I would make to this setup is that the operation would probably go more smoothly if there were a much narrower opening in the router table. An opening of almost but not quite zero clearance would be highly desirable.

If you haven't used a profile before, cut a sample piece before cutting good stock, especially when the good stock is relatively scarce material like the ⁵⁄₄ mahogany shown in the illustrations. (⁵⁄₄ wood is wood that is 1¼ inches thick.) In fact, it is a good rule in general to cut a sample piece first.

While it may not be necessary when making simple moldings against narrow openings, a featherboard like the one shown in Illus. 6-33 might prove a useful accessory when making complex ones. Even with a featherboard like the one shown in Illus. 6-33 in place, use a heavy-duty push stick. You don't want your hands anywhere near a cutter this big!

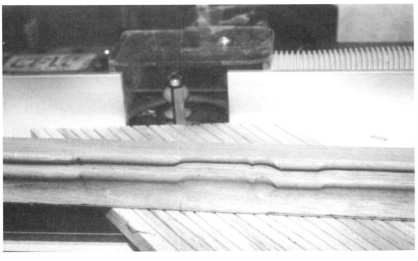

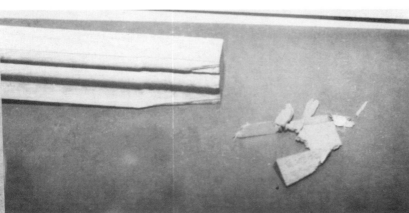

Illus. 6-34. The bigger and fancier the cut, the more important is a steady, smooth feed. A second's hesitation has rendered sections of this piece unusable.

Illus. 6-35. The large fragments of wood torn off the end of this piece show lots of reasons for making much more molding at a time than you think you need.

The bigger and fancier the cut, the more important is a steady, smooth feed. A second's hesitation has rendered the piece shown in Illus. 6-34 unusable. The large fragments of wood torn off the end of the piece in Illus. 6-35 is testimony that you should make far more molding at a time than you think you need.

Chapter 7

CUTTING AND ASSEMBLING A BASIC FRAME

Here are the procedures for cutting a basic frame from wooden stock rather than from pre-made frame stock and then assembling it:

1. Cut the stock to width and thickness. Clamp or fasten your miter box to the workbench to keep it rigid; also, the base to which you fasten the miter box makes it far easier to clamp the tool in place. Cut with long, steady strokes with little or no downward pressure. Let the weight of the blade do the work. Don't use short, jerky strokes, which often lead to errors that produce unacceptable cuts. Use a clamp to hold the work in place when your free hand isn't enough, but be careful that the clamp doesn't press so hard on the wood that it mars it (Illus. 7-1).

2. Apply any decorative edges.

3. Sand the piece (Illus. 7-2).

4. Cut a rabbet from what will be the inside edge of the molding. I cut in a range from ¼ inch wide × ¼ inch deep to ⅜ inch wide × ½ inch deep, but have settled on a ¼-inch-wide × ½-inch-deep rabbet as ideal for my framing work. Using the first piece as a setup gauge, it never takes more than one extra pass in each direction to get the cut right.

5. Now, apply the stain, varnish, lacquer, or other finish to your frame stock. This is the best time to apply the finish. Be sure to finish the inside of the rabbet edges, especially if the project is a frame for a mirror.

6. With the miter gauge set precisely at 45 degrees, cut one end off each piece of prepared stock, with the rabbet edge being the inside edge.

7. Determine the length of the piece as follows:

If the width of the rabbet in Illus. 7-3 is known (it is ¼ inch as discussed in step 4), then subtract A from the desired length—measure to the inside edge A^1. Once A is known, then A^2 minus A^1 is the correct length to add to each end of your outside edges. This

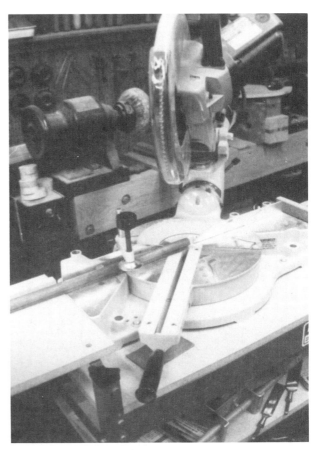

Illus. 7-1. Clamp the work in place.

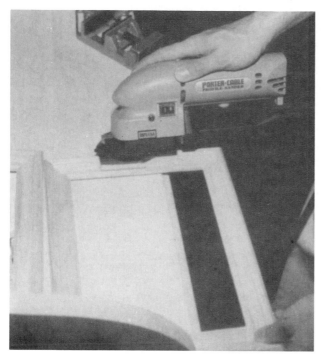

Illus. 7-2. Using a Porter-Cable detail sander to sand the actual profiles on a frame.

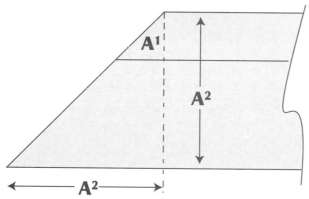

Illus. 7-3. Determining the length of the picture frame. The line shows how much to add to each length.

you cut must be an exact duplicate of the first. If you don't cut it exactly the same length, make it longer. A little bit can always be trimmed, but there's no

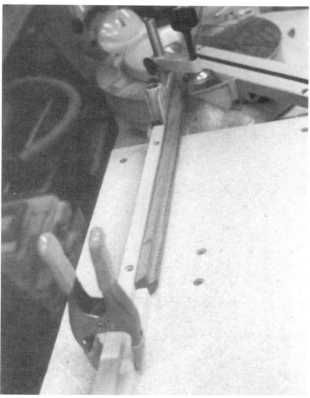

Illus. 7-4. Clamp stock blocks in place so that all matching sides come out the same length.

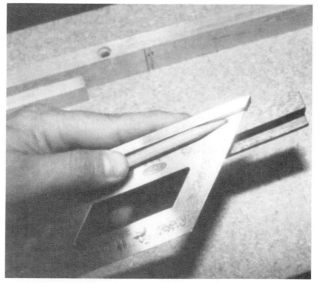

Illus. 7-5. Use a 45-degree "square" to mark the piece for cutting.

arithmetic can also be used to check your 45-degree "square."

8. With a sharp pencil, draw a pair of straight lines that bring both edges of your saw blade down to the front of the table. The more carefully you do this, the more accurately the lines will help you to make your cuts.

9. If your miter gauge doesn't have stops, clamp something in place (Illus. 7-4). The second piece

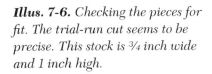

Illus. 7-6. Checking the pieces for fit. The trial-run cut seems to be precise. This stock is ¾ inch wide and 1 inch high.

way to add material. When setting up for this cut, you might use a 45-degree "square" so you have an exact line to which to cut (Illus. 7-5).

10. Cut the second pair of sides. These are fairly easy to set up. For example, if the long side of the picture frame is 3 inches longer than the short side, mark the gauge and move it 3 inches in the appropriate direction.

11. Check that the pieces fit (Illus. 7-6).

12. Adjust the pieces. Adjustment can be made with a tool like Pootatuck's Lion Miter-Trimmer. (See Chapter 3.)

13. Add glue (Illus. 7-7 and 7-8). If the material is already finished, you can use quite a bit of glue if you wipe it up right away. Even factory-cut pieces may not be precise, so using lots of glue (but keeping a wet rag handy) and maybe the appropriate type of brad-hole putty is important. Always touch up the

Illus. 7-8. Apply the glue liberally.

joints with glue, etc., and then wipe it off. The extra glue makes the joints stronger.

14. Clamp your pieces together (Illus. 7-9 and 7-10). Choose your framing clamps from those described in Chapter 3.

Illus. 7-7. Put glue on each mating surface, to ensure that the glue doesn't fail.

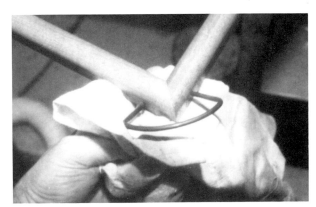

Illus. 7-9. The sample frame is assembled with spring clamps.

Illus. 7-10. With the spring-clamp pliers, remove the clamp after the glue has dried.

15. Remove all the sawdust so that all the pieces sit perfectly flat when you start nailing (Illus. 7-11).

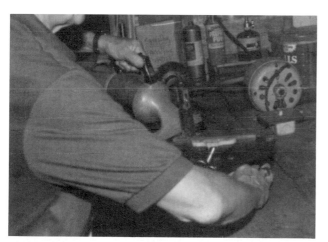

Illus. 7-11. After sawing the pieces but before nailing them, vacuum up the sawdust so that everything sits perfectly flat when you nail the pieces together.

16. Nail the corners together (Illus. 7-12 and 7-13), preferably at cross angles. This way, if the glue fails, you have a strong mechanical bond. Some professional framers assemble the frames with 3d finish nails and a hammer. For large frames Ron Stokes, a professional framer, applies two nails in one direction, one against the other, with glue in the joint. Finish the material before mitering it together.

Illus. 7-12. Drill a pair of holes for the brads with which you'll assemble the frame.

Illus. 7-13. Nailing the brads into the corners.

Illus. 7-14. Countersinking the nails with a nail set.

17. After countersinking the nails with a nail set (Illus. 7-14), put putty in the nail holes.

18. Burnish the edges of the mitered joint with a round metal edge, like the side of a screwdriver or of an awl (Illus. 7-15). The picture frame is now complete (Illus. 7-16–7-18).

Illus. 7-15. *Burnishing the edges of the mitered joint.*

Illus. 7-16. *A pile of shop-made frames that are ready to use.*

Illus. 7-17. *The woods should match better than this at the corners.*

Illus. 7-18. *The frame should be flat. This frame is out of square by a quarter inch over its 10-inch length, which renders it useless. The only way to salvage this frame would be to recut it at its corners and reassemble it in a smaller size.*

Assembling "Invisible" Wooden Frame Corners

As you become a proficient framer, you'll want to use wooden frames without having to patch one or both sides of each corner. Depending on your means, there is a pair of not very expensive machines for assembling wooden frames invisibly. These are the Cassese joiners (Illus. 7-19). Cassese

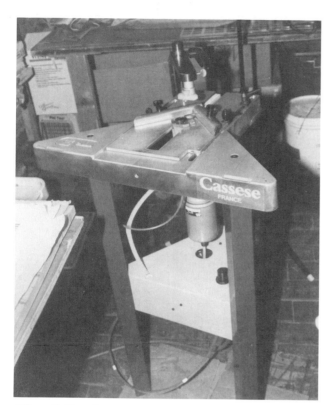

Illus. 7-19. The Cassese CS89 joiner in a workshop.

joiners are used to insert metal or plastic components under considerable force. If you're an occasional framer, neither of these is a tool that you'll need, but if you are interested in learning how professionals make frames or have become proficient enough to do some commercial framing yourself, one of these machines might be very useful to you.

The Cassese model CS88 joiner is foot-operated, so it requires no compressor. Like its pneumatic counterpart, the CS89, it takes less than 30 seconds to set up to cut a new molding. It has self-adjusting plungers for the widest possible variety of molding styles, adjustable miter angles, and tilting fences. It joins softwood or hardwood with ease. Its adjustable foot pedal allows the machine to be operated from the back, left, or right.

The Cassese model CS89 joiner has all the features of the CS88, and is enhanced by a powerful pneumatic cylinder for greater speed and ease of use. Like the foot-operated model, it has optional accessories for joining hexagonal- and octagonal-sided frames. While the foot-operated unit is intended for shops that frame from 5 to 12 pieces of

art per day, the pneumatic model is for shops that make from 8 to 20 frames per day. The pneumatic model also features an air regulator, an air safety button, and an on/off air switch.

Both models operate similarly, except in the step that fires the clamp and wedge (Illus. 7-20–7-24). With either, be sure the machine is against a worktable of the same height, to support any size frame and facilitate joining. Use a strong woodworking glue like Titebond. Adjust the sliding molding clamps for molding width. Use the quick-release handles to set the two wedge placement stops. Us-

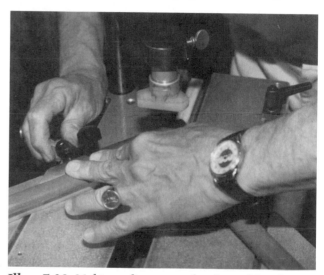

Illus. 7-20. Making adjustments for the molding by hand.

Illus. 7-21. Holding two frame pieces in place just before applying the wedge.

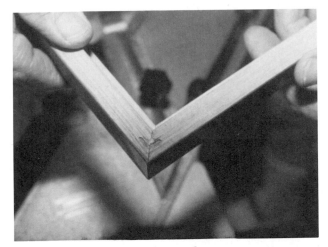

Illus. 7-22. *The first wedge in place.*

Illus. 7-23. *Commonly, two wedges are used in each corner.*

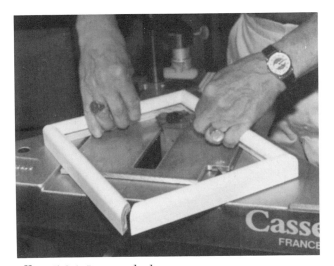

Illus. 7-24. *Joining the last corner.*

ing the quick-release handle, set the plunger within two inches of the top of the molding. With the foot-powered model, depress the foot pedal to engage the molding clamp and fire the wedge; on the pneumatic model, the foot pedal's first position sets the pneumatic clamp, and the second fires the wedge.

Both Cassese machines have lots of adjustable parts, so they can be made to work with a frame no matter how sloppy the fit is. There's nearly always a bit of doctoring to do. Always slop glue over the outside of the joints, and then wipe it off (Illus. 7-25 and 7-26); the extra glue makes the joints stronger. As with any machine, clean out all the places where glue might have dripped (Illus. 7-27 and 7-28), and then coat the mechanism with something like WD40 oil to keep it ready for the next use.

Illus. 7-25. *Slobber glue all over each corner.*

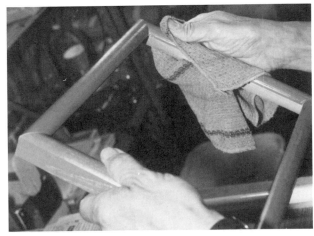

Illus. 7-26. *Wipe the excess glue off quickly.*

Illus. 7-27 and 7-28. As with any machine, as soon as you are finished using it, clean and lubricate it so that it will work accurately next time.

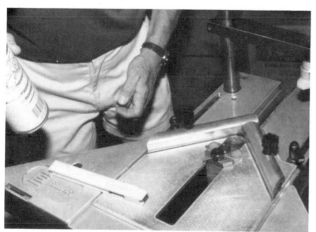

Illus. 7-28. Lubricating the Cassese joiner.

Frames You Can Open

Sometimes you want to frame an item in such a way that you can have easy access to it (Illus. 7-29). This happens to me when I'm framing magazines, pamphlets, and book covers. I enclose the material behind the glass or Plexiglas with a backing piece of Masonite, thin plywood, or whatever other thin stock is at hand, and hold the assembly in place with turn buttons, which also act as wall-protecting bumpers. The process of making such a frame is as follows:

Illus. 7-29. Checking the size of a picture frame.

Method #1

1. Make frame stock (moldings) per the instructions in Chapter 6.

2. Cut rabbets in the frame stock. Make the rabbets ⅛ or ¼ inch deeper than needed, to accommodate the rigid back you will be applying.

3. Cut your miters to appropriate lengths.

4. Glue and clamp the stock together. The new polyester glues are perfect for framing, and spring clamps are just about ideal; use wax paper to keep

Illus. 7-30. Spring clamps are ideal for a project like this. Note the wax paper being used to keep glue off the woodworking bench.

any excess glue off the woodworking bench (Illus. 7-30). Using the wax paper may be doubly important if you're framing at the kitchen table!

5. Remove glue squeeze-out from the frame's picture-holding rabbet. A skewed chisel is ideal for the squeeze-out.

6. Cut your glass and backboard to size.

7. Clean your glass and insert it.

8. Insert your mounted artwork (mat, filler, etc.).

9. Lay a cut-to-size sheet of backing behind the item being framed to fill out the opening, and then, with an awl, mark for the turn buttons (Illus. 7-31).

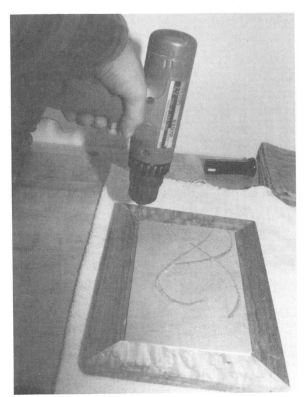

Illus. 7-32. Drill holes for the turn buttons' screws.

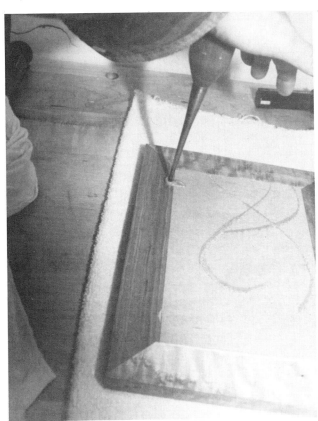

Illus. 7-31. Lay a cut-to-size sheet of backing behind the item being framed to fill the opening. Then, with an awl, mark for turn buttons.

10. Drill holes for the turn buttons' screws (Illus. 7-32). In some materials this won't be necessary.

11. Screw in the turn buttons with a manual or cordless screwdriver (Illus. 7-33). I find it useful to use the cordless model whenever possible. The turn buttons and unsealed back permit quick access, al-

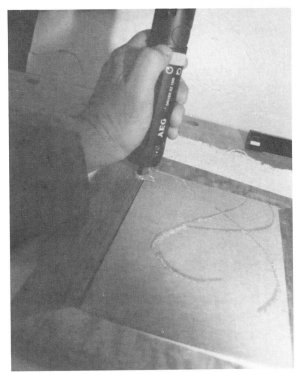

Illus. 7-33. Fill in the turn buttons with a manual or cordless screwdriver.

though they may not provide as perfect a protection as do sealed frames.

12. Attach the hanger hook near the top center of the frame and use a picture hanger, perhaps a decorative one, to hang the completed frame on the wall (Illus. 7-34).

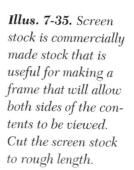

Illus. 7-35. Screen stock is commercially made stock that is useful for making a frame that will allow both sides of the contents to be viewed. Cut the screen stock to rough length.

Illus. 7-34. Attach a hanger hook near the top center of the frame. Next, use a picture hanger to attach the completed project to the wall.

Method #2

If you need a more protective frame that can be opened and that will allow both sides of an item to be viewed, you may be somewhat more limited in your choice of material. One commercially made stock that is particularly useful is common "screen stock," which is approximately 1⅝ inches wide × almost ⅝ inch thick (Illus. 7-35 and 7-36). With a router or with the dado head in your table saw, cut a dado as near to dead center as you can (Illus. 7-37 and 7-38). The width of the dado should be precisely the same as the thickness of the artwork and the covers on both sides. It can be cut either before or after the miters have been cut, but you'll lose less stock by cutting the dadoes after the material has been mitered (Illus. 7-39 and 7-40). Be sure to paint or stain

Illus. 7-36. A useful application for screen stock.

Illus. 7-37. Marking the center at the end. Set the depth of cut on the saw. I set the depth of cut for ⅜ inch, but ¼ inch would have been enough.

Illus. 7-38. Measure the thickness of your assembly. Mine is approximately ³⁄₁₆ inch. Make a centered saw pass.

Illus. 7-39 and 7-40. Cut the miters. Use flip-flops to match lengths. This will ensure good fits.

Illus. 7-40.

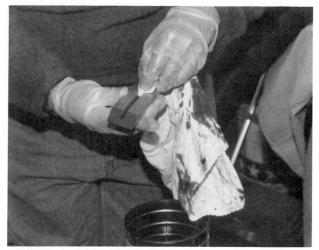

Illus. 7-42. *Adding a finish to the slot.*

the dado so that the bare wood in the channel won't be visible (Illus. 7-41 and 7-42). After the finishing materials have dried *completely*, assemble your whole insert.

The frame being made in this example is for a $3 note issued by the 1773 Continental Congress (Illus. 7-43). The objective is to make both sides of this old, rather fragile collector's piece visible. The note is protected from any detergent residues that might

Illus. 7-41. *Finishing the project. On a project like this, it is especially important to finish the slot, because if you don't it will be very visible. Small projects like this one can be dipped into the finish and then brushed with it if you're using a relatively clear finish such as finishing oil.*

Illus. 7-43. *The completed project. A $3 note issued by the 1773 Continental Congress is being framed.*

be left on the glass by absolutely neutral currency-collector's glassine, which, in turn, is mounted between two pieces of glass. By using small screws on the underside of such a frame, you are ensuring ready access to the note at all times, but, more important, you have also ensured that your framed note is protected in normal room conditions.

Chapter 8

CHOOSING AND CUTTING MATS

Mat board is a heavy-paper board from which you cut mats and backing boards. It can be obtained from most art-supply shops or framing shops. One of your local professional framers can sell you cutouts from the mats he or she cuts or can custom-order mat board for you.

Mat board is available in many different patterns and colors, and also in different compositions. It can be acid-free, 100-percent rag, or regular. (Rag is cloth converted to pulp for making paper. The finest mat boards are made of paper with very high rag content). Regular mat board has an acid-free core and backing, but the top colored paper can still be acidic.

Figuring out how to cut and mount mat board is actually quite easy after you figure out which type of mat board you're going to use. One supplier suggested that she had approximately 500 choices, and her selections all came from only one of several ven-

dors. Have an idea of what type and color mat board you want when you begin shopping for it. I counted literally dozens of shades of white when I went shopping. When I narrowed the selection to Vanilla Ice Cream, I was still shown quite a few choices. Catalogues from vendors are an ideal way to sample the wide variety of mat boards.

If you can find the pattern you want in the "cutoffs" bin at your local art-supply shop, you may get a real bargain. I paid less than $3 for two pieces of mat board approximately 16 inches wide × 20 inches long, which were more than big enough to make primary and secondary mats for the frame I had in mind. Primary mat is the piece of mat that touches the art. The secondary mat is between the glass and the primary mat. Though the primary mat is most often white, the secondary mat will often be colored (Illus. 8-1 and 8-2).

Now that you have the mat board, you need some-

Primary mat

Secondary Mat

Illus. 8-1. *A primary mat is the one that touches the artwork. The secondary mat is closer to the glass than the primary mat.*

Illus. 8-2. Primary and secondary mats.

thing to cut it with. A large-capacity plastic-scoring knife or a utility knife is just right to cut the material to size (Illus. 8-3). In the days when the beveled edge of the inside of the mat board was cut with a razor knife of some kind, cutting mat board was much more difficult than it is now. Today, there is a variety of mat cutters on the market that greatly simplifies the process. Professionals use complicated machines that take a long time to set up. These machines are very expensive, ranging in cost from $1,000 to $1,500. For cutting only a few mats a day, there is no reason not to use a relatively inexpensive, uncomplicated mat cutter like the Fletcher Terry MatMate System. I recommend the MatMate 40-inch system (Illus. 8-4) rather than the 32-inch system because it has a measuring scale built into the

clamp, measuring stops, and 8 inches of extra capacity (Illus. 7-4). This mat cutter also comes with very clear instructions.

A less expensive system that might accomplish the same function is the Alto 4501 mat-cutting

Illus. 8-4. The Fletcher-Terry Mat-Mate 40-inch system has a 40-inch cutting capacity and a solid cutting base. The system includes the Mat-Mate cutter, an adjustable straight-edge mat-board clamp, and a MatMate template for cutting beveled circle mat openings, marking mat borders, and measuring stops for the more accurate cutting of mat openings.

system. This reliable, easy-to-use system will also help in *designing* mats. The unique dimensioning system and detailed instruction manual enable users to design, lay out, and create a wide variety of cuts. The head can be used with a left- or right-hand pushing action (Illus 8-5), and it cuts a true 45-degree bevel, exposing more of the mat core to pro-

Illus. 8-3. A utility knife (right) is the perfect tool to use to cut the material to size. A plastic-scoring tool will also prove helpful.

Illus. 8-5. The cutter head on the MatMate 40-inch system swivels to both left and right.

duce professional-looking mat windows. The open-ended base unit is 8 × 32 inches and will cut any size mat with a border width of up to 6⅜ inches.

Even less expensive is the Logan Team System 1 Mat Cutter. This push-style mat cutter is intended for use by the occasional framer. The 24-inch guide rail has a rubberized nonslip base that securely grips the mat board. Its channeled aluminum design allows the cutting head to hook on and glide smoothly along the mat board. A dual U.S./metric scale makes measuring easy in either system. The cutting head makes beveled cuts only. It has a retractable blade holder for accurate entry, allows for an adjustable cutting depth, and has a start and stop indicator to help control overcuts.

Most professional framers wouldn't consider using models as basic as those just described. The Fletcher MatMate illustrated in this book is a system that will grow with the user. If, on the other hand, you feel that expense is no object, you can buy a mat cutter that costs several times that of the Fletcher MatMate without gaining much of an advantage.

Cutting Mats with the MatMate System

The instructions for using the MatMate system are as follow: Put a blade in the cutter so that the blade aligns with the white index mark on the cutter cover (Illus. 8-6). Then place the machine on a flat table surface so you can stand or sit at one end with the mat guide on the left. The mat guide can be pulled upward so it projects above the base. The end caps on the base have serrations (teeth) which engage matching teeth at both ends of the clamp. These teeth are ¹⁄₁₆ inch apart (2 millimeters in the metric system). So, to create a 2-inch border, put the clamp on the base so that its left edge is aligned with the 2-inch mark on the scale at both ends of the base. The teeth will hold it in place. Test the blade position by placing the mats together and making a cut

Illus. 8-6. *The MatMate's cutter head in place on the clamp, which guides it.*

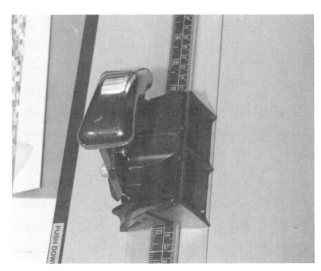

Illus. 8-7. *Here the MatMate cutter has the riser blocks which permit the straight cutting of the outside edges of the mats.*

(Illus. 8-7). The blade should cut all the way through the top mat and about halfway through the lower one. Place a scrap piece of mat (about 5 inches wide and 30 inches long) on the machine to prevent cutting into the base. This is called a "slip sheet." Lay a pre-sized mat board upside down on the slip sheet and slide it to the left against the mat guide. Draw a pencil line using the left edge of the clamp as a guide. This line should stop about 1 inch from the edges of the mat. Rotate the mat 90 degrees, position it against the mat guide, and draw another line

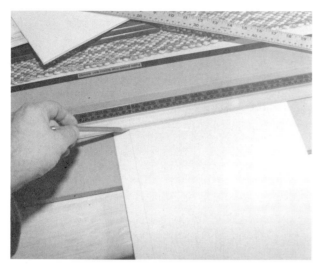

Illus. 8-8. Use the straightedge of the Fletcher-Terry MatMate to lay out your mat.

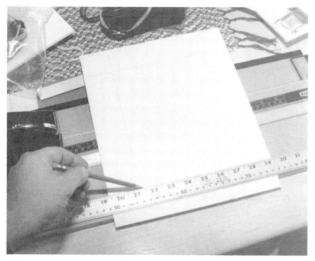

Illus. 8-9. You can also use a straightedge such as a ruler to lay out your mat.

(Illus. 8-8 and 8-9). Do this two more times so the cutout you want is outlined.

Place the cutter on top of the clamp with the blade to the left. Slide it until the index mark on the back of the cutter is positioned over the nearest pencil line. There are two index marks, each with an arrow showing the direction of cutting. Since you will push the cutter to make these cuts, use the index mark which has the arrow pointing away from you. Place your left finger and thumb on the tabs to keep downward pressure on the cutter. Rotate the cutter handle to insert the blade into the mat as far as it will

go. Slowly push the cutter until the index mark on the blade cover reaches the pencil line farthest from you. Rotate the mat 90 degrees and reposition it against the mat guide. Make another cut, starting and stopping at the pencil lines as before. Repeat this for the remaining two sides, and remove the mat and the scrap "fallout." The fallout should completely separate from the mat without the need to cut the corners too much. If it doesn't separate, finish the cut by hand using a spare blade. Change the start or stop position of the next mat you cut to be sure you have cut just enough to free the fallout.

If you prefer to use the MatMate system left-handed, simply turn the base 180 degrees so the mat guide is on your right. Now, you can either push or pull the cutter with your left hand.

Three locator pins are provided which allow you to position the clamp accurately. They fit in the holes in the end caps at both ends of the base. For example, if you wish to cut 2-inch borders, place the locator pins so the clamp rests against them at the 2-inch position. This will ensure that both ends of the clamp are at the same dimension. The holes are spaced ¼ inch apart; however, by rotating the locator pin one half turn, you can move the clamp ⅛ inch. The locator pins on the metric system move ⅖ inch (10 millimeters) from hole to hole; if you rotate the locator pin one half turn, they will move ⅕ inch (5 millimeters).

With the MatMate system, you size a mat as follows: Place the cutter on top of the riser and attach it with the two thumbscrews provided. Push the mat guide down until it is flush with the base. Place the slip sheet on the base, and then place the mat board, on which you have penciled lines where you want to cut, on the base. Position the clamp so its right edge is at the arrow points printed on the end-cap scales. When you use the riser, the blade must be extended farther. Loosen the knurled nut on the blade cover and slide the blade so it will penetrate deeper. For regular mat-board thickness, the end of the blade should line up with the end of the cutter cover. It should go completely through the mat and about halfway through the slip sheet.

Place the cutter on the clamp and position the mat so the blade will cut exactly on the pencil line. Proceed to cut the mat. Realign the mat so the blade will cut on the next pencil line, and make the next cut. Normally, you would expect to use two adjoining sides of an oversized mat, so only two cuts are required. Be sure to reposition the blade in the cutter when you remove the riser or you will cut too deeply on the next bevel cut.

The MatMate 40-inch system includes two measuring stops which are useful when you cut many mats of the same size with the same opening; for example, if you need to cut a number of 11-inch-wide × 14-inch-long mats with 2-inch borders. Place a measuring stop on the clamp at the 2-inch dimension on the clamp scale (Illus. 8-10). Lock it with the twist lock pin. Since you will start at the low end of the scale, you will be pushing the cutter right-handed. Place the clamp on the base for a 2-inch border. Put one of the mats in place against the mat guide and make four pencil lines along the left edge of the clamp. Slide the mat so it rests against the end cap with its 14-inch side against the mat guide. Start the cut with the cutter against the measuring stop. Proceed to cut, stopping when the index mark on the blade cover aligns with the opposite pencil line, as you did when making the first cut. Hold the cutter in this position and lock the other measuring stop against the body of the cutter. Turn the mat 180 degrees and cut the opposite side. Proceed to cut all of the mats on the same two long sides.

Next, put the first mat with the pencil lines in po-sition against the end cap with the 11-inch side against the mat guide. Start the cut with the cutter against the starting measuring stop as before, and stop when the index mark on the blade cover reaches the far pencil line. Now, reposition and lock the upper measuring stop against the cutter as you did in the previous step. You can now make all the short cuts in all the mats.

Also included with the MatMate 40-inch system is the MatMate Template (Illus. 8-4), which is used to cut beveled circle openings from 1 to 11 inches in

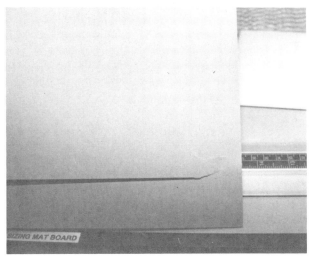

Illus. 8-11 and 8-12. Use a razor to cut corners if you're a little short with the mat cutter. You'll notice from these two illustrations that what you get if you just "tug" is an ugly tear and a piece of mat board that is ready for a garbage can!

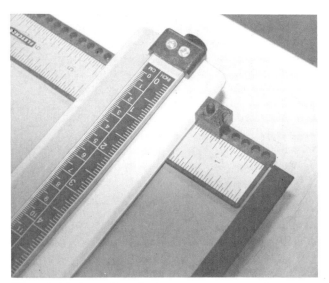

Illus. 8-10. Note that the MatMate's arm can be very accurately positioned and locked down.

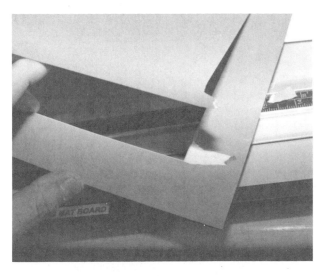

diameter. Additionally, you can use it as a guide to draw pencil lines on a mat from 1 to 6 inches from an edge. To draw these lines, turn the template upside down on the back of a mat. Place the rib against the edge of the mat. Use a sharp pencil and put it in the hole in the middle row where you want the line. Guide the template along the edge of the mat while holding the pencil against the mat. These holes are spaced ¼ inch apart and marked every 1 inch for your convenience.

Double Matting

Double matting consists of using a primary and a secondary mat on the artwork. The primary mat is the only mat to touch the artwork. It is nearly always white. The secondary mat is the one you see. It is more likely to be the same color as the art, to enhance it. The reason both mats have the same outside dimension is that if the glue that attaches them to the frame fails with the passage of time, one of them won't slip into the frame.

To cut double mats, first, use a ruler to measure the artwork's width and length, to determine what size mat you need to cut (Illus. 8-13 and 8-14). You should allow an approximately ¼–½ inch overlap all

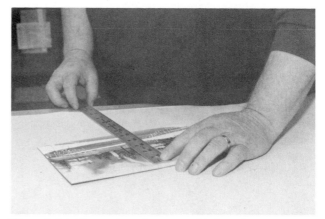

Illus. 8-14. Measuring the artwork's length.

the way around the artwork. In the example photographed for this section, the artwork is 10 inches wide, so taking it in ½ inch for the overlap makes it 9 inches wide. Add 5 inches for the mat, 2½ inches all around each side.

Mat board is cut to frame-size dimensions with a paper cutter or a razor knife. Bring the mat board to the mat cutter and set it in at the width you want to cut (Illus. 8-15 and 8-16). If you want a 2½-inch margin, set the mat cutter for a 2½-inch spacing. After you have set this margin, draw the knife smoothly from one end of the setting to the other (Illus. 8-17 and 8-18). Plunge the blade into the sur-

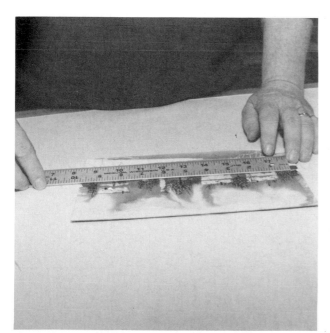

Illus. 8-13. Measuring the artwork's width.

Illus. 8-15. Bring the mat board to the mat cutter.

Illus. 8-16. Set the cutter to the width of the mat you wish to cut.

Illus. 8-17. Draw the cutter's knife along the platen from one end of the platen . . .

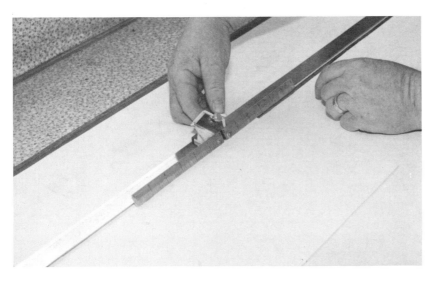

Illus. 8-18. . . . to the other end of the platen.

Illus. 8-19 and 8-20. Turn the mat board 90 degrees and repeat the process.

Illus. 8-20.

face, 2½ inches from one end, and push it to the 2½-inch mark at the other end. Turn the mat 90 degrees and repeat the cut (Illus. 8-19 and 8-20). Two more such turns and cuts complete the task. Sand the inside of the mat lightly a stroke or two to remove any fuzz left by the cutting (Illus. 8-21). This produces a bevel-edged mat with equal borders on all sides.

Always handle the mat board by its edges to prevent ugly fingerprints (Illus. 8-22). Oily fingerprints won't show up for four to six weeks, and then they'll become progressively uglier with the passage of

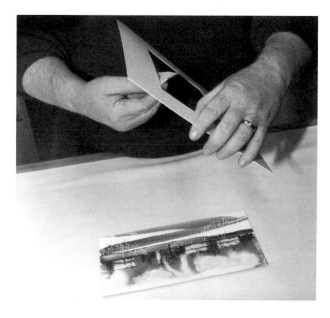

Illus. 8-21 (right). Sand the inside of the mat lightly a stroke or two to remove any fuzz left by the cutting.

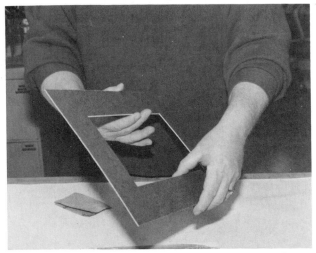

Illus. 8-22. *Always handle the mat board by its edges to prevent ugly fingerprints.*

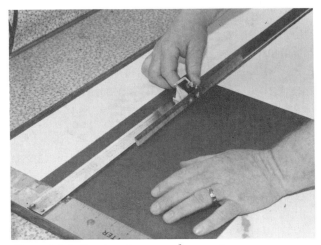

Illus. 8-24. *Cutting the secondary mat.*

time (Illus. 8-23). It may be possible to wear latex gloves while matting and framing, but the best approach is to work carefully.

Illus. 8-25. *Cutting the secondary mat.*

Illus. 8-23. *The fingerprint at the top center of the mat shown here didn't show up until the project was at least 10 years old.*

The secondary mat for this project is also cut to 10 inches wide by 14 inches long, so cut it ¼ inch narrower all around (Illus. 8-24–8-26). This ¼-inch margin is preferred by some picture framers, but it could be ⅛ inch, ¾ inch, or another dimension. Since the outside measurements are the same for both mats, they should line up perfectly after they have been cut.

Next, use an automatic tape gun to dispense two-faced tape at the top edge of the primary mat and

Illus. 8-26. *Cutting the secondary mat.*

also on the artwork (Illus. 8-27). Position the mat board carefully over the art (Illus. 8-28), and press it in place with the heels of your hands (Illus. 8-29). Now, the back of the artwork looks as shown in Illus. 8-30.

Next, use the automatic tape gun to spread a single strip of double-faced tape along the top of the secondary mat to hold it to the primary one (Illus. 8-31). The edges should line up perfectly (Illus. 8-32). This can be determined visually rather than

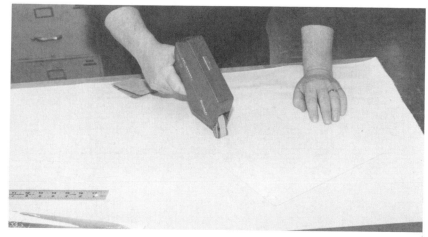

Illus. 8-27. *Use an automatic tape gun to spread a row of double-sided tape along the top edge of the frame.*

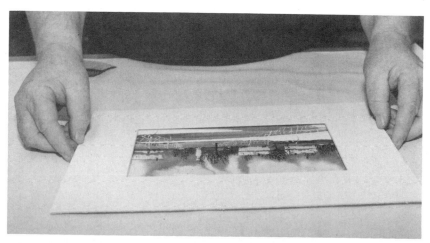

Illus. 8-28. *Position the mat board carefully over the art.*

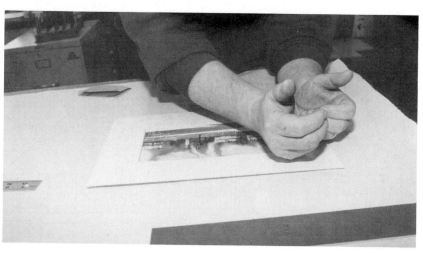

Illus. 8-29. *Then press the mat board in place with the heels of your hands.*

Illus. 8-30. *Now, the back of the artwork looks like this.*

Illus. 8-31. *With the automatic tape gun, spread another row of adhesive along the top of the secondary mat.*

Illus. 8-32. *The edges should line up perfectly.*

with a ruler. Immediately after dropping it in place, press the secondary mat down with the heels of your hands (Illus. 8-33). The finished assembly should look as shown in Illus. 8-34. If you're framing your own paintings or photos, sign them at this stage. If you sign them too soon, you may end up hiding the signature with the mat or making it too prominent by placing it too far from the actual edge.

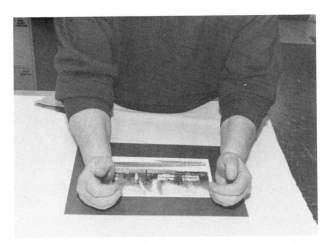

Illus. 8-33. *Immediately after dropping the secondary mat in place, press it in place with the heels of your hands.*

Illus. 8-34. *The finished artwork looks like this.*

Note that the artwork is only loosely attached to the primary mat (Illus. 8-35). Now, cut a piece of 2-inch stock from the material the artwork is made of (Illus. 8-36). Attach this backing to the artwork on the back with the automatic tape gun (Illus. 8-37

Illus. 8-35. *Note that the artwork is only loosely attached to the primary mat.*

Illus. 8-36. *Cut a piece of backing that will fit under the artwork on the back.*

and 8-38). Now, if the glue fails, the mats won't slip down into the frame. The piece is ready to mount to the picture frame.

Cutting Curved Openings in Mats

Curved, mainly circular, openings in mats can be simply cut by using the MatMate Oval/Circle Mat Cutter that comes with the MatMate 40-inch system described earlier (Illus. 8-39–8-41). If you are

Illus. 8-37 (right). *With the automatic tape gun, attach this piece of filler.*

Illus. 8-38. Attaching the filler.

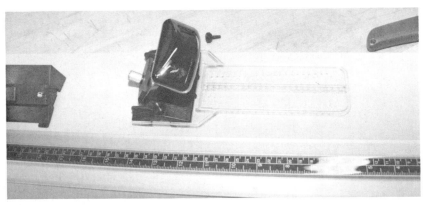

Illus. 8-39. The Fletcher-Terry MatMate template, included with the MatMate 40-inch system, can be used to cut beveled circle openings from 1 to 11 inches in diameter. In addition, you can use it as a guide to draw pencil lines on a mat one to six inches from an edge.

Illus. 8-40. This top view of the MatMate Oval/Circle Mat Cutter shows the blade-mounting mechanism and the adjusting head.

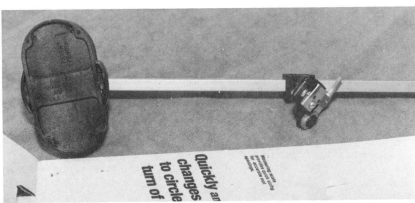

Illus. 8-41. A bottom view of the MatMate Oval/Circle Mat Cutter.

going to cut more than an occasional arch or circle, you'll want a tool more like the MatMate Oval/Circle Cutter, which cuts beveled edges from 4¼ to 24 inches high and circles from 4½ to 21 inches in diameter. The tool's design allows you to switch from cutting ovals to circles with just the turn of a knob.

There are other optional accessories that can be used to cut curved openings. To use the curve cutter shown in Illus. 8-42, exchange the rectangular blade for a pointed one, mount the cutter head on the template, set the pivot pin in the middle of the curve to be cut, and guide the cutter head around the appropriate curve.

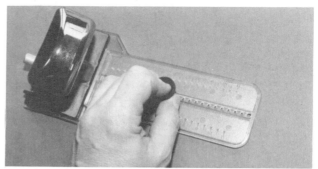

Illus. 8-43. Insert the pivot pin in the hole corresponding to the desired diameter and into the mat at its marked location.

Illus. 8-42. The Logan 3 Step Oval & Circular Mat Cutter is one of the many options for cutting circular mats.

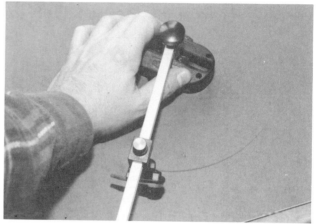

Illus. 8-44. Cut as far as you can, and rotate the mat and its scrap piece to a position where you can continue the cut.

There are three rows of holes in the template. The middle row will be used for drawing pencil lines. The two outer rows are used for circle-cutting. An arrow at the end of each row identifies whether that row is used to cut clockwise or counterclockwise. Mark the center of the circle to be cut on the surface of a mat board. Place the mat face up on a larger piece of scrap mat. Insert the pivot pin in the hole corresponding to the desired diameter and into the mat at its marked location (Illus. 8-43). Hold the pivot pin firmly in position so it does not slip out of the mat. Gradually pivot the cutter handle to insert the blade into the mat while rotating around the pivot pin. Cut as far as you can, and rotate the mat and its scrap piece to a position where you can continue the cut (Illus. 8-44). Be sure to leave the blade and pivot pin in the mat. When you complete the cut, bring the cutter handle to an upright position

and remove the cutter, template, and scrap fallout from the mat.

If you will be cutting many curves, you will appreciate the Fletcher-Terry MatMate Oval/Circle Mat Cutter, which cuts ovals with beveled edges from 4½ to 24 inches high or circles from 4½ inches to 24 inches in diameter. You can turn a knob on this device to adjust the scale from cutting ovals to circles in seconds; no tools, additional parts, or assembly are required. An exclusive tracking-guide wheel automatically keeps the cutting blade on track throughout the entire cut to create bevel openings without start and stop marks.

When using these and other similar accessories, it is important not to let the base shift while cutting and rotating the mats. It is also necessary to keep slight downward pressure on the beam to be sure the blade remains fully inserted in the mat. Do not push down on the beam too hard, or scuff marks may appear on the mat. You may notice a track mark on the mat caused by the device's tracking wheel; this mark is in the scrap fallout, and is normal. Practice a few times on the scrap mat to make it easy to keep the cutter base in place, and gradually insert the blade with your other hand while turning the beam. Always use a sharp blade; Fletcher-Terry supplies blades in packages of 10 and 100.

On most of the projects you frame, you're likely to be cutting a curved edge into a square-edged piece of mat board. If you're actually making a round or elliptical mat, be sure to cut the outside of the piece first, so that you have a firm center against which to cut the inner piece.

Cutting Larger Circles

Here's how to cut larger circles. With a pencil and ruler, lay out and mark the center of the part of the mat board to be cut. Draw X's on the board to ensure accurate location of the mat-cutter's center (Illus. 8-45–8-47). Draw the tool around the circle or arc before cutting (Illus. 8-48), just to be sure that you're actually cutting what you mean to. With pressure on the cutter, swing it through approximately half the arc (Illus. 8-49), and then change hands to complete the circle (Illus. 8-50). If you've cut deeply enough, the cut center should lift out easily (Illus. 8-51). With some sandpaper, remove all the rough edges from the newly cut mat (Illus. 8-52), and then dust the area with a piece of paper towel (Illus. 8-53). Finally, if you can find a tool like the

Illus. 8-45. Setting up the mat to cut it.

Illus. 8-46 and 8-47. With a pencil and ruler, lay out and mark the center of the part of the mat board to be cut. Draw X's on the board to ensure accurate placement of the mat-cutter's center.

Illus. 8-47.

Illus. 8-48. *Draw the tool around the circle or arc before cutting it, to ensure that you're actually cutting the area you want to cut.*

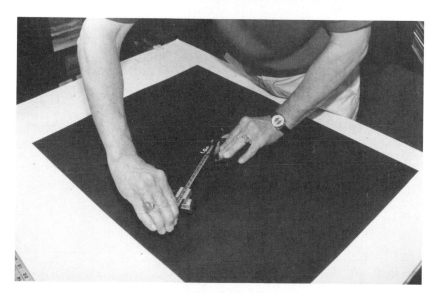

Illus. 8-49. *With pressure on the cutter, swing it through approximately half the arc.*

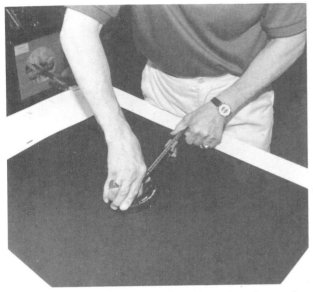

Illus. 8-50. Then change hands to complete the circle.

Illus. 8-52. With some sandpaper, remove all the rough edges from the newly cut mat.

Illus. 8-51. The cut center should lift out easily.

Illus. 8-53. Dust the area with a piece of paper towel.

"bone" shown in Illus. 8-54, use it to burnish your newly cut edge. Only one additional step remains: To minimize waste, cut the rounds off the edges right away, so that you'll have a square to use on one of the next small projects you frame (Illus. 8-55 and 8-56).

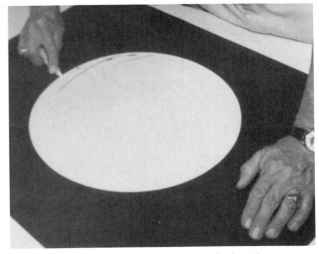

Illus. 8-54. Using a "bone" to burnish the edge.

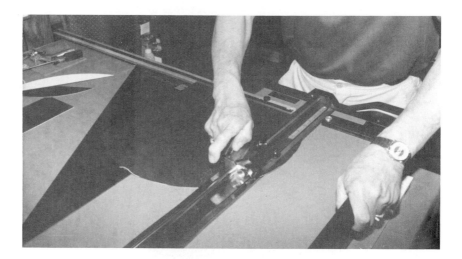

Illus. 8-55 and 8-56. To minimize waste, cut the rounds off the edges right away, so that you'll have a square to use on one of the projects you frame.

Illus. 8-56.

Illus. 8-57. The artist with the completed circular mat.

Illus. 8-58. The assembly ready for framing.

Illus. 8-59 (above left). No matter how carefully you work, an arched top mat like this one is likely to have a wiggle in it. **Illus. 8-60 (above right).** It is better to cut an arch with a corner like the ones shown in this photo.

Chapter 9

SELECTING AND CUTTING GLASS

Glass is used to protect the artwork. You can either cut your own glass or buy pieces from your local glass merchant. It's not necessary to learn to cut glass for picture-framing, especially for basic picture-framing, because there's no real saving in buying large sheets of glass rather than pieces cut to size by your local glass merchant, who cuts it from 4-feet-wide × 8-feet-long sheets. On the other hand, knowing how to cut glass permits you to reuse frames no longer being used or broken or flawed sheets of glass.

More important than cutting glass is knowing what kind of glass to choose. *Picture-framing* glass is ¹⁄₁₆ inch thinner than regular glass, but you'll find that using *regular single-strength window glass* for most common framing needs is more economical. In 1995, I paid $4.50 for two pieces of window glass, one 11 inches wide × 14 inches long, and the other 9 inches wide × 24 inches long, so this glass will not prove costly. Conservation glass reduces glare while at the same time keeping all ultraviolet light away from the artwork. Generally speaking, conservation glass will be at least twice as expensive as regular picture-framing glass, which in turn will be markedly more expensive than good, modern window glass. Some viewers believe that nonglare glass has as many disadvantages as advantages. Loss of clarity is the most common complaint, but in many locations you may have to sacrifice some clarity to prevent glare or reflection. New glass is clearer than old glass, which is more likely to have bubbles and ripples that distort accurate viewing.

The TruVue Company (1315 N. North Branch Street, Chicago, Illinois 60622-1919) offers four top-quality glass products designed for framing. Its Premium Clear is ideal for glossy prints and photos, matte-finish photos, and posters. Its Reflection Control is ideal for needle art, matte-finish photos, and posters. There are two grades of conservation glass (Conservation Clear and Conservation R.C.), which are good for original art, needle art, matte-finish photos, and heirlooms. (Conservation Clear is also good for glossy prints and photos.)

Cutting Techniques

The materials needed to cut glass include a bottle of mineral spirits, glass cleaner, a wooden ruler, a marker, and, of course, a glass cutter (Illus. 9-1). Clean the glass before cutting it, to ensure that there is nothing on it to damage the glass cutters. Clean it by washing it with regular window-washing soap. The first time the tool skips, it should be discarded. A skip will create a "break" in the glass other than along the line you intend to score.

Observe the following procedure when cutting glass: First, wash your hands to protect it from fingerprints. Then place it on a flat, cushioned surface in preparation for marking it. Clamp one end of the ruler in place. A spring clamp will work well. When marking, or scoring, the glass, pull the glass cutter toward you, using the ruler as a guide. Make one firm, clear stroke and run the line off the edge of the glass (Illus. 9-2). This doesn't take much pressure. You'll hear a "sizzle" when you cut the glass. Don't score it a second time. If not breaking it right away, turn it over so the marks don't get rubbed off.

To break the glass, grip it on both sides of the scored line (Illus. 9-3), twist it outward (Illus. 9-4), and snap it in half cleanly and deliberately (Illus. 9-5), using the corner of the table as your guide. Break the glass within two minutes of scoring it. If you are not satisfied with the cleanness of the break, the next time brush kerosene on the cutting line before running the cutter down it.

Next, clean the glass to remove all cut particles. Use clear water first to remove all the big chunks of

Illus. 9-1. The materials used to cut glass include a bottle of mineral spirits, glass cleaner, a wooden ruler, a marker, and a glass cutter.

Illus. 9-3. Grip the glass on both sides of the scored line.

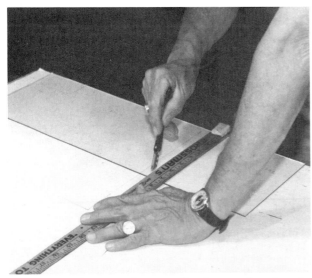

Illus. 9-2. Clamp a ruler over the glass to the edge of the worktable, hold it at the other end with your hand, and draw the glass cutter along the ruler. Only one pass is required.

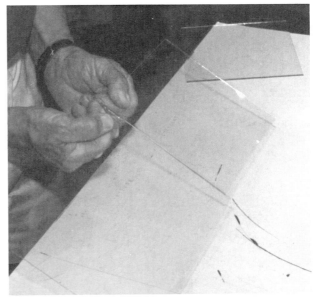

Illus. 9-4. Twist the glass outward.

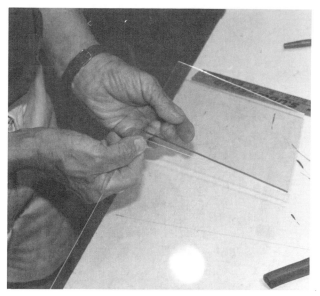

Illus. 9-5. *Twisting the glass outward snaps the pieces apart.*

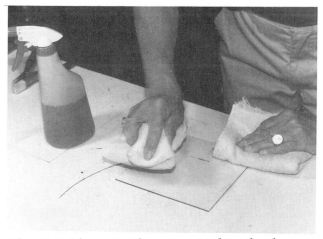

Illus. 9-7. *After using clear water to clean the glass, use a light spray of glass cleaner.*

dirt. If the glass is small enough, the best place to wash it is in a sink (Illus. 9-6).

Then use a light spray of glass cleaner (Illus. 9-7). Dry it with a soft towel (Illus. 9-8) and inspect it for cleanliness (Illus. 9-9).

After cutting and cleaning the glass, be sure to sweep the glass shards away from the work space

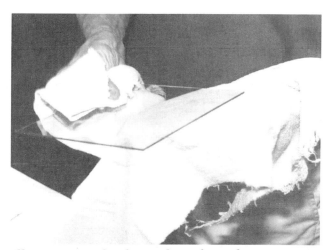

Illus. 9-8. *Dry the glass with a soft towel.*

Illus. 9-6. *If the glass is small enough and if there's a sink handy, that's the best place to wash it.*

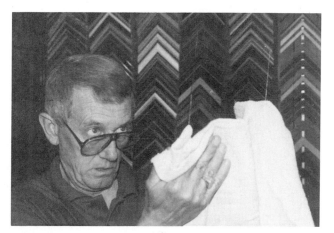

Illus. 9-9. *After toweling the glass dry, inspect it for cleanliness.*

(Illus. 9-10). Then insert the glass directly into the frame, to protect it (Illus. 9-11). If you are not using it immediately, store it upright in a place where it won't be broken.

Using Plexiglas

An alternative to using real glass is to use Plexiglas—which is acrylic plastic sheets. Plexiglas is used in applications where glass must be very light (as when framing large artwork), when the framed product must be shipped, and when the glass has a greater chance of breaking. Plexiglas also has a higher attraction for static electricity, so it works as a dust magnet. For this reason, it should not be used to

Illus. 9-10. After cutting glass, be sure to sweep the glass shards away from the work area.

Illus. 9-11. Inserting the glass directly into the frame.

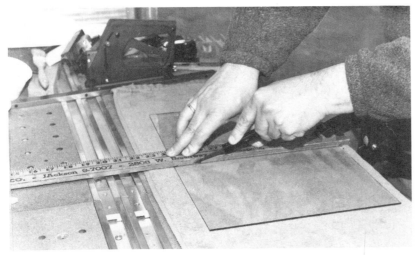

Illus. 9-12. Scoring Plexiglas with a plastic-cutting tool.

house artwork that is made with pastel, charcoal, or other media that have the potential to attract dust. There are posters in my office that were very satisfactorily framed with Plexiglas years ago. The only disadvantage Plexiglas has in comparison to regular glass is that it has a higher risk of being scratched.

Plexiglas must be scored several times with a plastic-cutting tool like the one shown in Illus. 9-12 before it is snapped. Plexiglas costs about half the price of top-grade framing glass. It comes with a sheet of protective paper stuck to it. Use the Plexiglas before this protective paper permanently sticks to it. There are sure to be projects for which you'll prefer to use Plexiglas.

Chapter 10

ASSEMBLING AND CLOSING THE WORK

After you have made the frame, cut the mat, and cut the glass, you are ready to assemble an artwork package and enclose it in the frame. Assembling the package consists of putting the glass, mat, art, and backing together. This has been put into a separate chapter because you will be assembling and closing the work whether you make or buy the frames, the glass, and the mats.

Illus. 10-1 shows all the supplies you need for closing a framed artwork: a ruler, a pencil, kraft paper, picture-hanging wire, screw eyes, bumpers, an awl, a wire cutter, an automatic tape gun, and a FrameMaster brad or point installer. Actually, a home framer who's working only occasionally won't necessarily need an automatic tape gun and brad installer. Instead, rubber cement can be used to laminate the kraft paper in place. Another option is to spread a bit of hot hide glue on the back of the frame and then press a sheet of kraft paper in place. Then,

after the glue has mostly set, sprinkle or spray a fairly liberal dose of water on the kraft paper; as the water dries, it will cause the paper to shrink, leaving it tightly fixed to the back of the frame. If an automatic tape gun is used, the paper will only be as tightly attached to the back of the frame as it has been pulled.

Here are the steps involved in assembling and closing the artwork:

1. *Burnish the frame.* There is some debate as to whether the frame should be burnished when it is actually being made, or at this, the assembly, stage, and whether the burnishing step is needed at all. Many professional frame makers choose to skip this step. While viewing an art exhibition recently, I marveled at how many otherwise handsome paintings, prints, calligraphies, etc., were marred because of the rough corners of their frames.

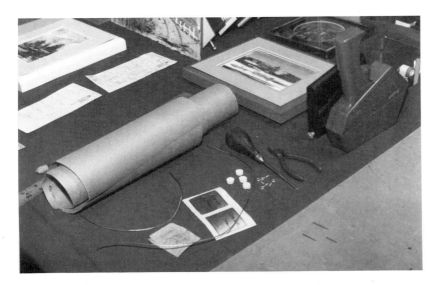

Illus. 10-1. *Shown here are all the supplies you need to assemble the artwork and enclose it in the frame. They include a ruler, a pencil, kraft paper, picture-hanging wire, screw eyes, bumpers, an awl, a wire cutter, an automatic tape gun, and a brad installer. Instead of the automatic tape gun, you can opt to use rubber cement or hot hide glue.*

Burnishing consists simply of making a couple of quick strokes on the frame with an awl or the side of a screwdriver (Illus. 10-2). This causes the wood fibers to lie down so that they more nearly meet each other. The few seconds it takes to do this makes your art much more attractive. You should burnish the corners of every frame.

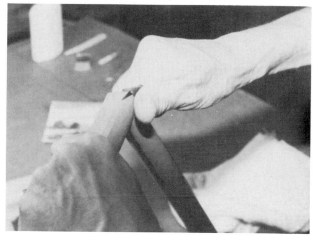

Illus. 10-2. Burnishing the corners of a wooden frame.

2. *Check the glass for dust or other unwanted objects.* If you find something, now is the time to remove it. Some conscientious framers have been known to disassemble an artwork package as many as half a dozen times in preparation for closing. If

Illus. 10-3. Using a FrameMaster brad installer to install the brads that hold the insides of the frame in place.

you find dust specks, lint, or other small particles on the enclosed glass, remove them.

3. *Install the brads in the back of the artwork.* It's not necessary to use a Fletcher-Terry Frame-Master point driver (Illus. 10-3) to do this. Indeed, if you frame only a project or two a year, you might be content with a tool like the much simpler Fletcher-Terry FrameMate brad installer or even to insert brads carefully with a pair of pliers (Illus. 10-4). When using brads, hold the brad in the pliers and press it into the molding material. After you have used the FrameMaster, you're sure to want one, and they are not much more expensive than a manual construction stapler.

Illus. 10-4. Brads can also be carefully inserted into a frame with a pair of pliers.

4. *Secure the kraft paper to the frame.* You first have to add a bonding material all around the back of the frame. You have three options: an automatic tape gun (Illus. 10-5), rubber cement, or hot hide glue.

Hold the kraft paper over the frame to check that they match in size, and then press the kraft paper into place, stretching it as tightly as possible as you go (Illus. 10-6). Then sand off the excess paper. This may sound as though it would take a great deal of time, but the operation is completed with just a few strokes of 220-grit sandpaper (Illus. 10-7). Burnish the edge with the awl that you've been using during this process.

Illus. 10-5. With an automatic tape gun, apply tape all around the perimeter of the back side of the frame.

Illus. 10-6. Pressing kraft paper in place. Stretch it as tight as possible while doing this.

Illus. 10-7. Sanding off the excess kraft paper.

5. *If using self-adhesive bumpers, remove the paper which protects the adhesive and stick the bumpers to the lower corners of the back of the artwork* (Illus. 10-8). While the bumpers permit a flow of air behind the entire framed work, which helps the work to last longer, there's no real necessity for them.

6. *Make the holes for the screw eyes that hold the wire.* Use the awl to puncture the holes (Illus. 10-9 and 10-10). After you have made the punctures, use the awl to more easily turn the screw eyes into the back of the frame.

Illus. 10-8. Using self-adhesive bumpers on the lower corners of the artwork's back.

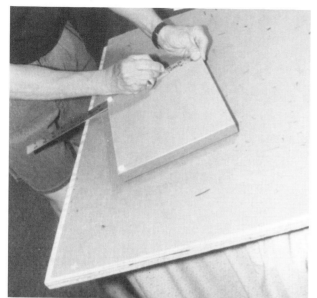

Illus. 10-9. Marking the holes for the screw eyes.

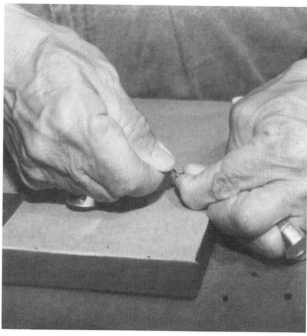

Illus. 10-11. Six winds of the wire are enough to hold it in place. There is no need to tie any knots.

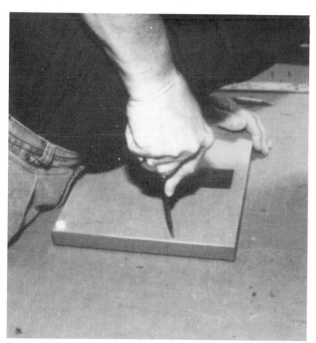

Illus. 10-10. Use an awl to turn the screw eyes into the frame.

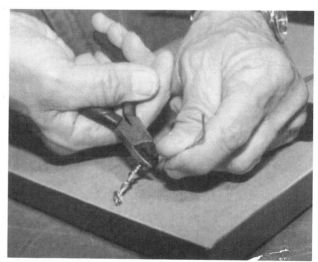

Illus. 10-12. Use a wire cutter to neatly trim away the excess wire.

7. *Run the wire through the eyes and wind six very tight revolutions around each end* (Illus. 10-11). This is enough to hold the wire in place, and there is no need to make any knots. Use a wire cutter to neatly trim away the excess wire (Illus. 10-12). The artwork is ready for hanging.

Assembling a Metal Frame

The procedures for assembling metal frames are only slightly different from those used for wooden frames:

1. Make sure that you have the proper hardware kit (Illus. 10-13 and 10-14). You can get the hardware kit from the supplier of your metal frame; the hardware kit should be included in the price of the frame stock. The hardware kit typically consists of four metal corner angles with inserted setscrews (which tighten the corners to the frame stock), four backing plate angles, eight spring clips (which hold the mat, art, and backing boards tightly to the front of the metal frame), two hangers with inserted setscrews, and two wall protectors (bumpers).

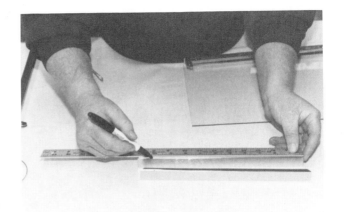

Illus. 10-15. Check the measurements of your frame.

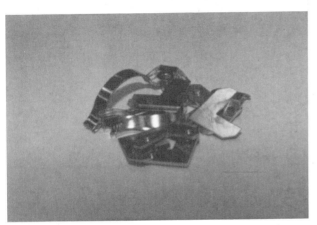

Illus. 10-13. The hardware kit that is used to assemble each picture frame.

Illus. 10-16. If necessary, use your miter box to cut the frames to their correct size.

Illus. 10-14. The kit consists of two plates. One of the plates has a pair of screws which spread the plates apart.

2. Check the measurements of your frame (Illus. 10-15).

3. If you have to cut the frame to its correct size, use a miter box (Illus. 10-16).

4. After cutting the frame, file it with a jeweler's file to remove the metal shards (Illus. 10-17 and 10-18).

5. Measure the piece of glass that will be used. If it is not the proper size, cut it (Illus. 10-19–10-24).

6. After cutting the glass, wash it (Illus. 10-25).

7. Sweep all the glass shards from your work area (Illus. 10-26).

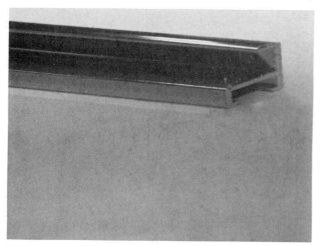

Illus. 10-17. *The frame will have metal shards on it after it has been cut.*

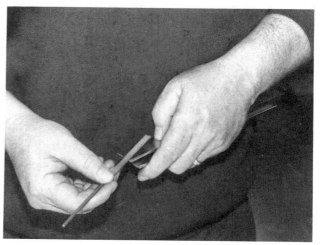

Illus. 10-18. *To remove the metal shards, file the frame with a jeweler's file.*

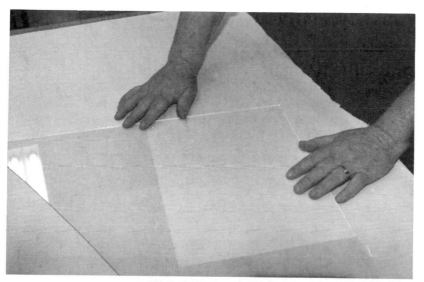

Illus. 10-19. *If you didn't buy your glass at exactly the right size, you will have to cut it. Insert a piece of backing material for this under the glass at one corner. This shows you exactly where to cut it.*

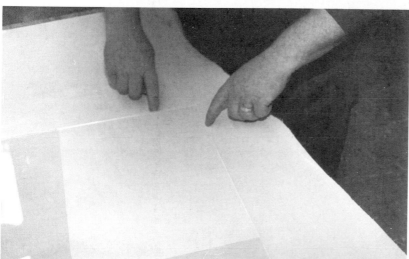

Illus. 10-20. *The properly positioned backing.*

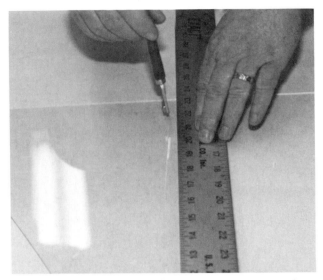

Illus. 10-21. Lay a straightedge (preferably backed with cork) on the properly positioned backing.

Illus. 10-22. The straightedge should be positioned along the visible edge of the backing.

Illus. 10-23. Draw the glass cutter along the straightedge.

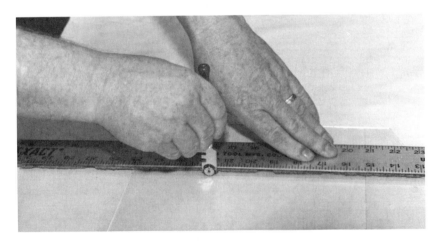

Illus. 10-24. Lay the marked score right along the edge of the table and give it a quick snap. To ensure that the break is clean, make the break within a moment or two of scoring the glass.

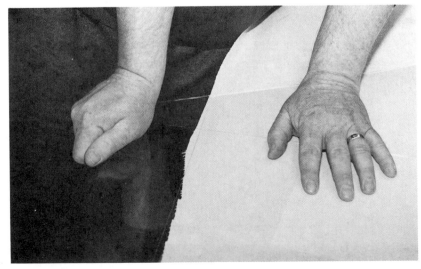

Illus. 10-25. *Washing the glass. Hold the glass with a corner of the wiping rag to ensure that you don't leave fingerprints on it.*

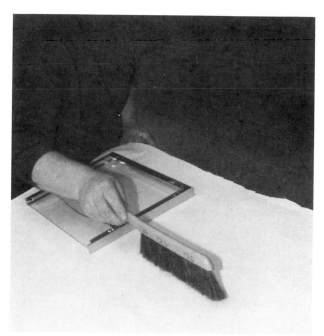

Illus. 10-26. *Sweep all the glass shards from your work area.*

8. Place the three sides of the frame together, and then attach the hanger hooks (Illus. 10-27 and 10-28).

9. Next, add the hanger wire to the picture frame (Illus. 10-29–10-34).

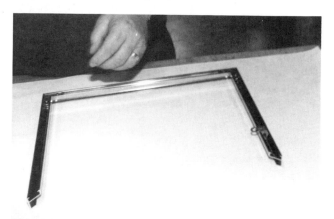

Illus. 10-27. *Place the three sides of the fence together and attach the hanger hook.*

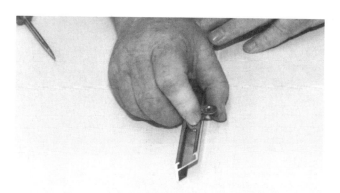

Illus. 10-28. *A close-up of the hanger hook.*

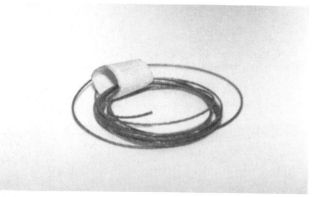

Illus. 10-29. *Store your hanger wire in a reverse-wound length of masking tape.*

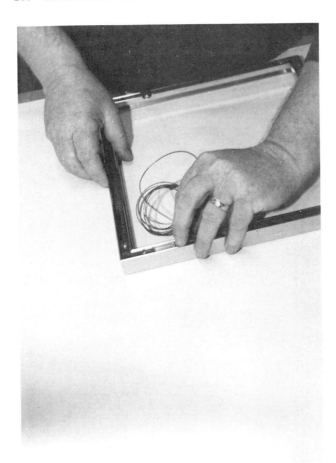

Illus. 10-30. Loop the wire through the hanger hook.

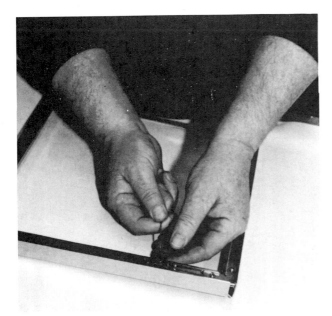

Illus. 10-31. Then twist the wire six times around the hook.

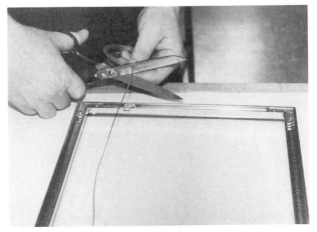

Illus. 10-32. Bring the wire past the other hook and cut it to rough length. Even a pair of common household scissors can be used for this cut.

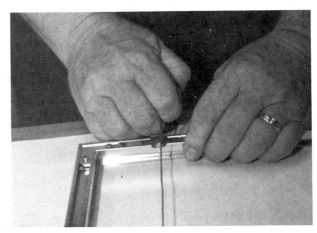

Illus. 10-33. Pull the wire tight through the second hook.

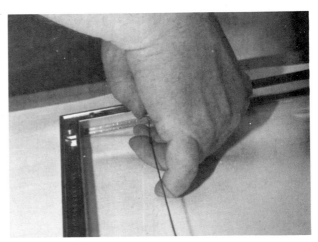

Illus. 10-34. Also give this side six twists.

10. Unfasten the top of the frame (Illus. 10-35) and remove it (Illus. 10-36).

11. Slide the frame over the glass (Illus. 10-37 and 10-38).

12. Add the assembly to the frame (Illus. 10-39–10-41).

Illus. 10-35. *Unfasten the top of the frame.*

Illus. 10-36. *Then remove the top of the frame.*

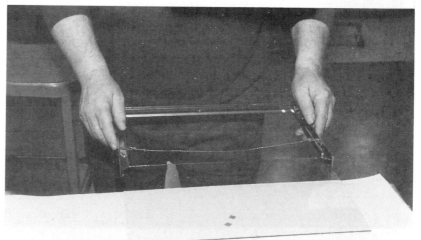

Illus. 10-37. *Set the glass so that it is slightly over the edge of the table, and slide the frame over it.*

Illus. 10-38. *As you turn the project up, holding it only by the frame, the entire glass enters the frame.*

Illus. 10-39. *Turn the frame 180 degrees so you can add the rest of the assembly.*

Illus. 10-40. *Put in the artwork and the related mats.*

Illus. 10-41. *Then put in the backing.*

13. Inspect the assembled project for fuzz or dirt and sweep the dirt from the frame (Illus. 10-42 and 10-43). To do this, you have to remove the artwork.

14. Reassemble the entire project (Illus. 10-44).

15. Add the clips (Illus. 10-45 and 10-46).

16. Finally, apply the bumpers (Illus. 10-47).

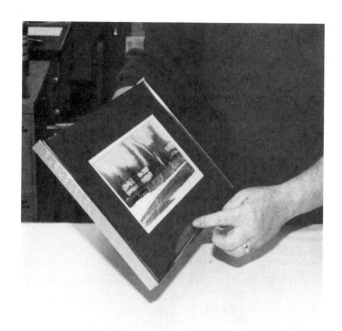

Illus. 10-42. *Turn the project over and inspect it for fuzz and dirt. There almost certainly will be some.*

Illus. 10-43. *Remove the artwork and sweep the offending particles from the frame. Do this as many times as necessary.*

Illus. 10-44. *Reassemble the entire project.*

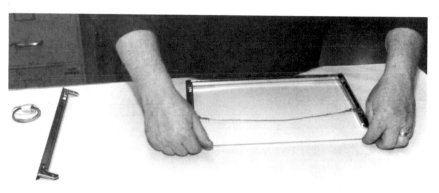

Illus. 10-45. *After screwing the top on, put the clips in place.*

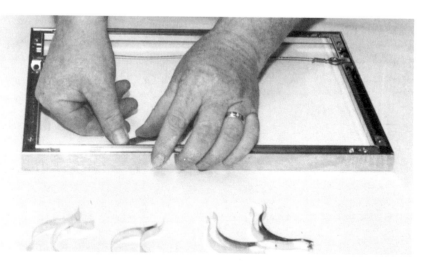

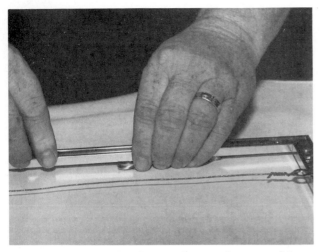

Illus. 10-46. *Slip the clips in place so that one of their edges protrudes slightly. If you do not do this, the assembly will not fit together properly.*

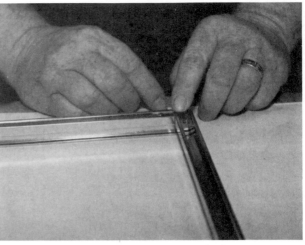

Illus. 10-47. *Apply the bumpers to the lower corners of the frame. The bumpers permit air to flow behind the artwork, which helps it to last longer.*

Chapter 11

HANGING FRAMED PICTURES

Hanging framed pictures is a very important part of the framing process. After all, the finished project has to look good hanging on the wall. If you have selected the right frame, it *will* look good if it hangs straight. Hanging picture frames on two nails will ensure that they will hang straight and evenly.

Follow these procedures when hanging picture frames: Measure the distance from the top of the frame to the top of the wire when the wire is stretched tight. Add that distance to whatever distance you want the picture to be from the ceiling. Measure this total distance from the ceiling to the center of the picture frame, as the picture frame was when you held it in place to see how it looked. This is done by setting a square right on top of the picture frame at its center to mark the wall above it. At that height, hang two fasteners, three or four inches apart. This pair of hooks will ensure that your picture frame hangs straight. The fact that there are two hooks for it to hang on may make the picture frame fractionally higher than your measurements indicated, but this distance will not matter.

Follow the same procedures when hanging one picture frame above another. Set a square right on the top of the first picture frame at its center to mark the wall, well above the first picture frame (Illus. 11-1). Measure now from the bottom of the second picture frame to the top of its stretched wire. Add the desired space between the picture frames. Mark the wall at an appropriate height above the first picture frame. Next, square to the ceiling, make two marks equidistant from the center and hang *two* hooks. If you question whether the picture frame is parallel to the ceiling, use a level to draw a line parallel to the horizon, to which the ceiling is nearly always paral-

Illus. 11-1. *Center a square on top of the first picture frame.*

lel; this way, the picture frame will be easy to straighten, and is more likely to stay straight. If you

Illus. 11-2. *Drill a pair of holes.*

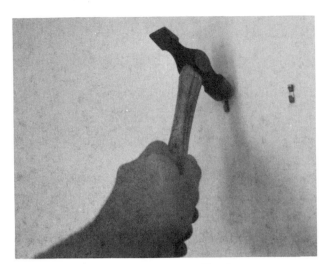

Illus. 11-3. Next, turn in a pair of hooks.

Illus. 11-5. These decorative fasteners add a nice touch to the picture frames.

Illus. 11-4. The net result is a properly matched pair of framed pictures like those shown here.

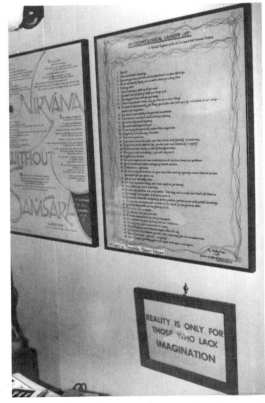

Illus. 11-6. This collection of posters brightens a basement office.

are drilling in Sheetrock or paneling, just hammer in the hooks. If you're mounting them in old-fashioned plaster, predrill each hole to prevent cracking the plaster and/or bending the nails (Illus. 11-2–11-4). Sometimes you'll want to use decora-

tive fasteners like those shown in Illus. 11-5.

When you're hanging artworks in a group, it's important to allow some extra space for picture frames of varying sizes (Illus. 11-6 and 11-7). It is also important to trust your own taste. If you finish a group-

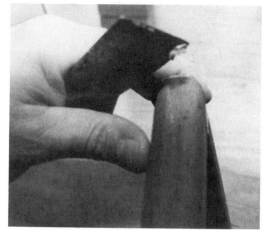

Illus. 11-7 (left). A collection of framed book and magazine covers. *Illus. 11-8 (above).* Plugging the hole on a hanger.

ing and don't like it, you can remove the hangers and plug the holes on white walls so that they are almost imperceptible with something as simple as plain white toothpaste. Another approach is to use a bit of Sheetrock cement (as a softer, less expensive alternative to spackling powder) and some paint to plug the holes (Illus. 11-8). Be bold. Try some picture-arranging ideas that you believe would work well.

TrackMaster

There is a new product on the market called the TrackMaster, which hangs metal- and wood-framed art simply, securely, and straight (Illus. 11-9). To install artwork with this frame (Illus. 11-10), simply hold the frame in its desired position on the wall and mark the wall, using the frame's top as a guide. Measure down and place the top of the hanger even with the bottom of the frame rail. Tap in the center nail. Insert the level vial into the hanger and pivot

it until it is level. Drive nails into the ends of the support track, and remove the level. For wooden frames, install the wood adapter, and then slide it towards the slot behind the frame's support track. Center the wood adapter on the top back of the frame and fasten it with screws. The positioning tabs should be snug against the frame. Place the adapter onto the support track, where it can be moved from side to side for positioning.

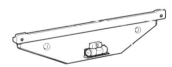

Illus. 11-9. The TrackMaster.

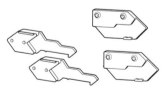

Illus. 11-10. How to use the TrackMaster.

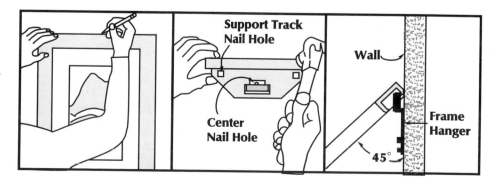

Chapter 12

PROJECTS

Needlework Project

Framing Needlework

For those who do needlework, a picture frame is a great way to show it off. Knowing how to frame your own work will save you a great deal of time and money.

The first step after completing the work is to wash it in a laundry machine. Let the project air-dry, pulling it together once in a while, if necessary, to ensure that it is basically square. If the needlework comes through the laundry cycle relatively square, all you'll need to do is press it with several passes of a steam iron (Illus. 12-1); the main objective here is to fill the work with steam so that you can tug it to square as much as necessary (Illus. 12-2). (Squaring or straightening the work is referred to as *blocking*.) If the work still isn't square, dampen it slightly and pin it to a board where you can steam and stretch it until it is square (Illus. 12-3).

Illus. 12-2. If the back of the needlework is as neat as shown here, the work is more likely to stay straight or square.

Illus. 12-1. Pressing the needlework with a steam iron.

Illus. 12-3. Needlework pinned to the board so it can be pressed with a steam iron and stretched before being mounted.

Illus. 12-4. Attaching the work to a piece of foam-core backing.

When the work is square, it can be attached to a piece of foam-core backing with double-sided adhesive tape or even an automatic tape-gun (Illus. 12-4). I try to do my taping on the back side of the foam core, so that if the adhesive comes loose, there is enough tension within the frame to keep the needlework from slipping down; having the fabric stretched over the top of the foam core really helps to ensure this. It would be possible to staple the work to the foam-core board or fix it in place with pins. A mechanical fastening would be preferable to just an adhesive mounting.

Illus. 12-5. Test-fit the work with a frame and mat before assembling the pieces.

As soon as the piece is mounted on the foam core, measure it to determine the dimensions of the mat, glass, and frame to be cut, and cut and/or order these pieces. When you have them, test-fit them together before assembling them (Illus. 12-5).

Freestanding Needlework Frame

Here is a relatively simple, small project that's perfect for displaying needlework (Illus. 12-6–12-12), and it can be done inexpensively and fairly quickly with a lathe and other ordinary tools. Furthermore, it is a project that lends itself to short production runs, and one that can be done in short, pleasurable sessions. If you can frame a picture in an evening, then you can build this handsome adaptation of a colonial fire screen in a couple of evenings, because it consists mainly of a framed picture—almost always needlework of some kind—mounted not on the wall, but on a rather handsome tripod stand. While these instructions are only for a single unit, I would not consider making fewer than three of them at a time because most of the actual operations are far less time-consuming than the set-ups for them.

The first step is to prepare for turning the spindle, which, of course, requires the use of a lathe. Since you probably can't purchase 4 × 4 stock locally, gluing pieces together seems unavoidable. If you book-match the pieces as you glue them (that is, put the pieces from the same face of the board together, so that the two edges nearest the saw cut come together), you are more likely to have a handsome spindle as a result. Plane the stock so that the ends of the pieces are only a few thousandths of an inch thicker than their middles, and the pieces will fit very well together. Glue the joint neatly with just enough clamping pressure, because the pieces should fit together so well the joint should not require much pressure.

After the glue has set, cut the stock to a hexagonal (six-sided) shape. Drill a ⅞-inch-diameter hole into one end of the piece; this end will hereafter be the *top*. Plug this piece with an easily removable plug; I used a dowel and hot-melt glue (as from a glue gun).

The dowel or plug does not have to be ⅞ inch in diameter. I use a ⅞-inch dowel because I happen to have a ⅞-inch Forstner bit and a plug cutter. The only thing to be concerned with is that if the plug is sturdy and looks good, then it will work.

Next, mount the spindle stock on the lathe. First, turn the hexagonal piece to a cylindrical shape with a 1½-inch-deep fluted long and strong gouge. Then turn the piece to its final shape. The spindle shape shown in the illustrations was improvised by me, but you can invent your own shape or copy one from your favorite source.

One caution about the spindle turning: Be sure to leave several inches on the bottom of the spindle

Illus. 12-6. A freestanding needlework frame.

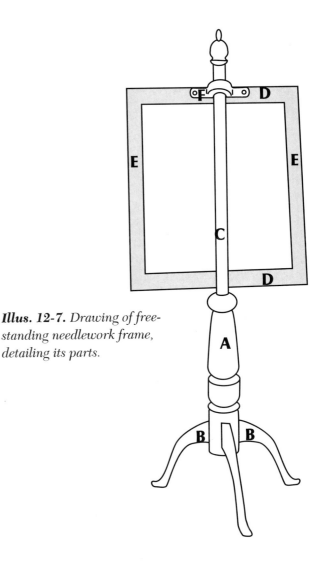

Illus. 12-7. Drawing of freestanding needlework frame, detailing its parts.

straight, rather than undulating, fluted, or otherwise highly figured. This is what makes it possible to apply the legs to the spindle.

After you have finished your turning and sanded it through 220-grit sandpaper, set the gauge on your lathe so that you can divide the sides of your now-

decorated cylinder evenly into thirds, each centered 120 degrees from the other parts. At each of these three spots, flatten a spot equal to the thickness and length of each of the legs. Cut the three legs now if you haven't already. Although I didn't supply a diagram of the spindle because I wanted to encourage

Cutting List for Freestanding Needlework Frame

Part Label	Piece	Quantity	Thickness	Width	Length
A	Spindle Blank	1	3½"	3½"	17"
B	Blank for leg (note grain orientation)	3	¾–1"	8"	8"
C	Dowel (length varies with frame size)	1	⅞"		26"
D	Frame top and bottom	2	¾"	2"	18¾"
E	Left and right frame sides	2	¾"	2"	21¾"
F	Frame mounting blank	1 or 2	1"	2"	6"
	Finial	1			
	Panel retainers/turn buttons				
	1¼" × #8 flat-head brass screws				
	⅝" × #6 flat-head brass screws				
	½" × #4 flat-head brass screws				
	5/16" diameter dowels				

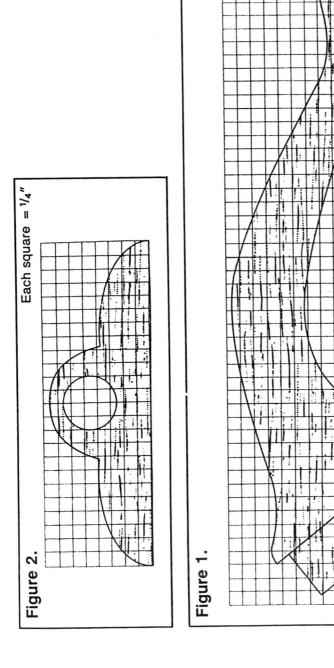

Figure 2.

Each square = 1/4″

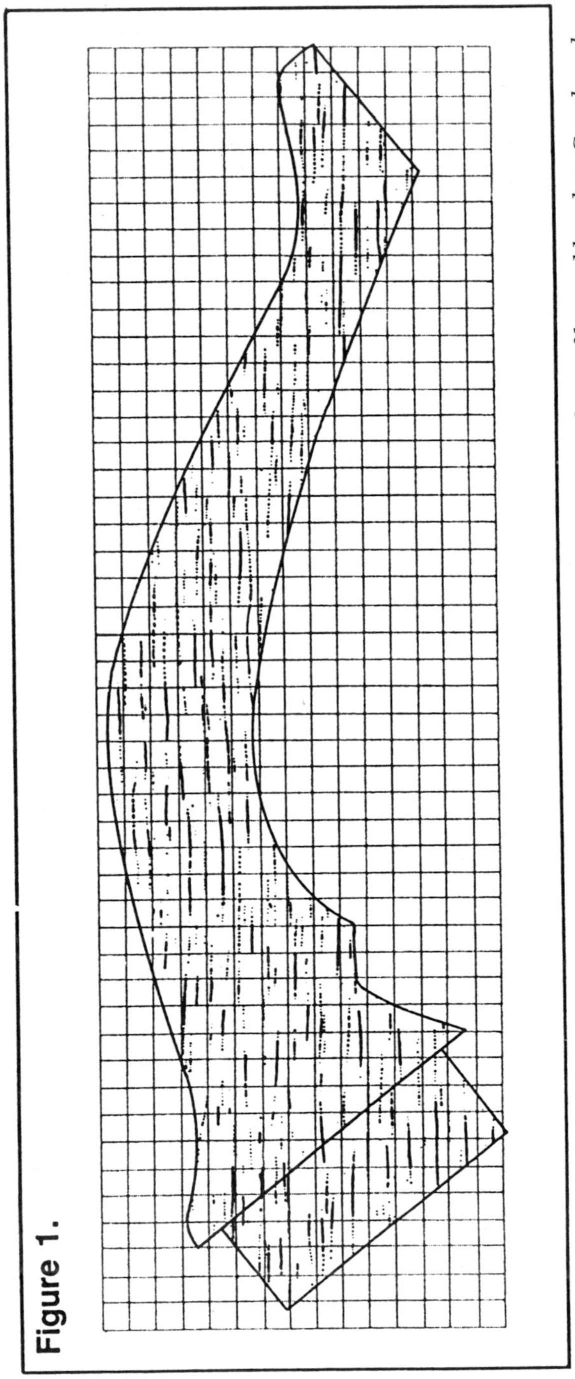

Figure 1.

Illus. 12-8. Templates of leg and bracket. Cut three legs.

Illus. 12-9. *A close-up of the tripod on the freestanding needlework frame.*

Illus. 12-10. *The bracket that mounts the frame to the post.*

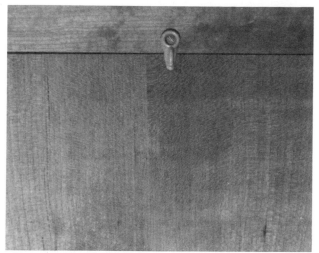

Illus. 12-11. *Turn buttons.*

Illus. 12-12. *Corner of frame.*

some experimentation and creativity, I am going to give a few specific hints about the kind of legs you should use on the project. Illus. 12-8 shows roughly the right shape and size; deviating too far from this could be an engineering blunder. The grain must run the length of the legs. It is best to cut a template and then to cut the remaining legs with a pattern-cutting router bit.

An alternative that I find attractive is to mark the stock with a template (Illus. 12-13–12-15), cut the legs on a band saw (Illus. 12-16), clamp them together, and shape them with files and sandpaper (Illus. 12-17). If this is your first tripod project, you may prefer to experiment with this second method;

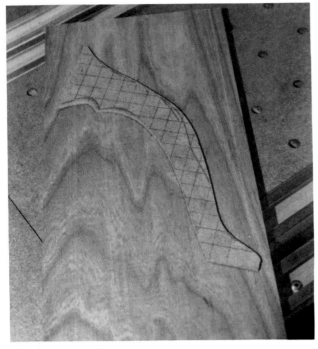

Illus. 12-13. A leg template.

Illus. 12-14. After laying out the leg, I use an angle gauge and a table saw to flatten the bottom of the feet and the portion of the leg that joins the spindle.

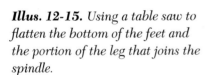

Illus. 12-15. Using a table saw to flatten the bottom of the feet and the portion of the leg that joins the spindle.

Illus. 12-16. Cutting the legs with a band saw is faster than using a scroll saw, but the band-sawn line will need sanding.

Illus. 12-17. *Sand with an electric sander or by hand.*

otherwise, the pattern-bit method is a good way to do it.

The leg pattern shown in Illus. 12-8 is for a dowel-mounted leg. Make sure that you flatten the three mounting locations so the thickness of the leg can be mounted flush. To mount the legs with dowels, do the following: Make a template with a piece of scrap stock that will permit you to drill the same pair of holes in the end of each leg that will be attached to the dowel (Illus. 12-18). Drill the holes. Put

dowel centers in each drilled hole. Press the leg against the appropriate spot on the spindle; the dowel centers will mark these spots for drilling. Be sure to drill these holes in the spindle stock straight (Illus. 12-19). Glue the dowels and the mating surfaces on the legs and spindle lightly and assemble them (Illus. 12-20). I have found that the assembled leg is too odd a shape to clamp, so I have used a quick-set glue and held each leg while the adhesive set. Neat gluing is essential, because cleaning up excess glue on these curved surfaces is nearly impossible.

Illus. 12-19. *Clamp your template and a leg between two pieces of stock. Then, perhaps using a clothespin as a depth stop, drill through the template with a handsaw. In this exercise, we are using a ⁵⁄₁₆-inch drill bit and ⁵⁄₁₆-inch doweling.*

Illus. 12-18. *Cut a piece approximately 1 inch wide from flat-edged stock left over from the legs. Use this piece as a template for drilling the dowel holes. Lay out for two dowel holes. Drill two at the drill press.*

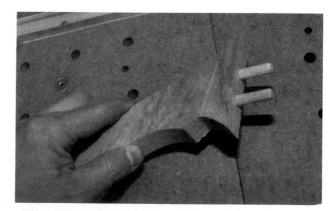

Illus. 12-20. *Then insert the dowels.*

After the adhesive has dried, remove the plug from the top. This should be a fairly simple matter of inserting a chisel and giving it a twist. Mount your 7/8-inch-diameter dowel; this can be bought or shopmade. I made my own, cutting an even 7/8-inch square on a piece of stock of the appropriate length, and then using a 3/8-inch roundover bit. The resulting dowel is not perfectly round, but it is close enough to be very attractive, and it is much less expensive than buying hardwood dowels in material other than birch.

Next, glue the dowel in place. At this time, fit but don't glue in the finial. Check the stand now to make sure it is level, and plane, sand, or file off the bottoms of the feet if they are not level until you are satisfied that the tripod is standing straight and true. Then make a frame-mounting bracket as shown in Illus. 12-10. To do this, start with a piece of 1-inch-thick × 2-inch-wide × 6-inch-long stock, drill a 7/8-inch-diameter hole, and then cut the piece to shape with a band saw. Then sand or scrape it finished.

Framing Method   With a router, shaper, or hand plane, create the edge shape you desire on the pieces to be used for the frame before you cut them to length. Cut them to the length and width of the framed item, plus a little more than twice the width of the frame stock (this excess is to allow for the stock taken up by the miter joints). Then set the saw fence to 3/8 inch and cut a rabbet or relief to hold the glass, matting, needlework, and backing material (which should be made of fine, thin plywood to match the material for the rest of the project). Cut the 45-degree miter roughly with your table saw's miter gauge; then trim the miter with a miter trimmer. Glue up your frame using any of the standard framing clamps.

Next, mount the back with turnbuttons, which are sometimes referred to as "panel retainers." Glue and screw "frame mounters" to the frame, and mount the frame on the stand with small brass screws. Next, glue or tack the finial in place at the top. Finally, add the matting and glass. Of course, the stand should get a couple of coats of your preferred finish before the needlework is mounted to it (Illus. 12-21). My stands received two applications

Illus. 12-21. *The completed project in use.*

of Danish oil, followed by a buffing with a fine furniture wax.

Try this piece or some variation of it. It will improve your design, joinery, and jig-making skills, and perhaps your mass-production techniques, without costing you much money.

Poster Frame Project

It seems that most of us collect posters and other artworks so quickly that we really don't know how to store or display them. Before I learned to make my own picture frames, I bought Poster Frames, by AFP Acme Frame Products, Inc., an American

Greetings Company. These frames (Illus. 12-22) have several advantages. They have a stiff cardboard backing; the white paper on one side of their edges masks the edges if the poster is slightly undersize; they have attractive hangers (that attach to the cardboard rather than to the frame); and they are made of thin but light and very serviceable Plexiglas. Unfortunately, there is also one serious disadvantage: the clip-on edges won't stay in place, and the bottoms won't stay on for long without regular attention.

Illus. 12-22. *These commercial frames, which can be clipped onto your posters, are inexpensive and attractive.*

For quick, very inexpensive short-term framing, these frames are fine, but for the longer term, metal frames, even at somewhere between three and four times the price, are really both a drastic improvement and very easy to use.

I recently decided to build a picture frame using Poster Frames and Nielsen moldings at my kitchen table. With no previous hands-on experience, I put together four precut metal frames from made-to-measure moldings, assembled the artworks (posters) into them, and had them ready to hang in under an hour, including the time it took me to shoot photographs of the process.

I had measured the posters and ordered precut black metal frames. These arrived a few days later, and I set the posters in their old frames on the kitchen table for easy disassembly. Then I screwed three sides of the new frames together, using the same Plexiglas and backing material as were in the original poster frames. For two of the posters, the assemblies just slid into the new Nielsen frame, but for the other two, some trimming of the Plexiglas and the backing material was required. To do this, I took the assembled posters to my woodworking shop and there I set up a straightedge along the actual edge of the poster. Then I used a Plastic-Plus Cutting Tool, shown in Illus. 12-23, to cut the Plexiglas to the size of the new frame (Illus. 12-24 and 12-25). I used a regular Stanley "handy knife" to cut the backing material along the same straightedge, and reassembled the now handsomely framed posters for remounting in my office (Illus. 12-26 and 12-27).

Illus. 12-23. *Use a tool like this to trim the Plexiglas to the size of the new frames.*

Illus. 12-24. *I clamped a ruler to the bottom edge of the actual picture and trimmed the actual Plexiglas.*

Illus. 12-25. *Trimming the Plexiglas.*

Illus. 12-26. *Make sure you attach the description of the artwork to the back of the assembly.*

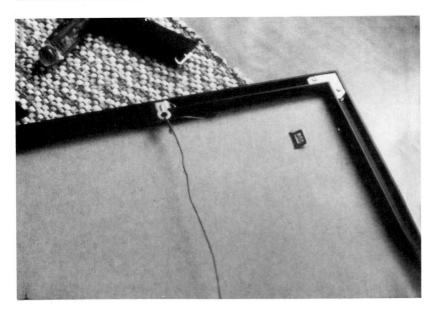

Illus. 12-27. *Attach the clips and the hanging wire.*

APPENDICES

GLOSSARY

Assembly of Artwork   Putting the glass, mat, art, and backing together before putting them into the frame.

ATG Tape   Double-sided tape used for double- and triple-matting, and used with kraft paper to keep the frame free from dust.

ATG (Automatic Tape Gun)   A dispenser for applying two-sided tape.

Backing   The substrate which supports the artwork. The artwork is held in front of the backing.

Backsaw   The cutting tool used in a hand-powered miter box. It has fine teeth and a stiff spine that supports the back.

Bevel   A slanted angle at which mats are cut.

Blocking   A method of stretching and/or shaping fabric (as in needlepoint, counted cross stitch, other fiber arts, or oil-painting canvas) into a straight shape for framing.

Brad   A thin nail with a very small head.

Bumpers   Usually self-adhesive corner protrusions added to lower-back corners of the frame to keep it straight on the wall and to prevent the framed art from rattling whenever the wall shakes.

Burnishing a Frame   Using an awl or the side of a screwdriver to make a couple of quick strokes on the frame. This causes the wood fibers to lie down so they more nearly meet each other.

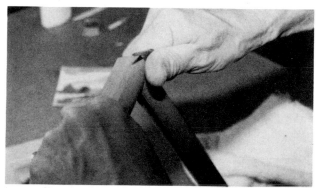

Burnishing the corners of a wooden frame.

Carcass   The basic frame or box of a cabinet.

Chop   Molding that has been precut/mitered to a specific size. Many companies that sell precut moldings limit their sizes to 4 × 4 inches for safety reasons. Most frame vendors give an allowance of between 1/16 and 1/8 inch unless you specify an exact measurement.

Corner Clamp (also called a miter clamp)   A device used to hold two sides of a frame while their mitered corners (usually at 45 degrees) are being glued and nailed.

Dado   A T-shaped joint that is used to make boxes, cabinets, and shelves.

Dry-Mounting   Attaching paper, cloth, or another material of artwork to a firm backing (foam core, Plexiglas, or substrate), using adhesives with heat and/or pressure.

Dust Cover   Usually kraft paper (like brown grocery-bag material) applied to the back of a frame with adhesive, to keep out dust and bugs.

Easel Backing   A backing used to support free-standing frames.

Filler Board   The last piece added to a frame before it is closed. It may be foam core, acid- and alkaline-neutral board, or mat board, but *not* regular corrugated cardboard because of its acid content.

Fillet   A decorative strip of wood, usually gold or silver in color, placed next to art or between mats.

Finishing   The process of giving raw wood its decorative or protective coating.

Applying a coat of varnish to molding as a finish.

Floating   A process of displaying art so that all its edges are visible.

Foam-Core Board   A lightweight board which is made of polystyrene sandwiched between two smooth papers. It is excellent for use as a backing or substrate.

Framer's Molding   Molding that differs from builder's molding because it has a built-in rabbet to hold glass and other components.

Framing Vise   A vise used to hold cut pieces at a 90-degree angle for accurate assembly.

Glass   The material used to protect the artwork in a picture frame. It is available in standard sizes. There are also different types of glass. Picture glass is thinner, less likely to have flaws, and more expensive than single-strength glass. Non-glare, non-reflecting glass is much more expensive and diffuses the image in some cases, but is useful, perhaps even necessary, in locations where there is a lot of glare.

Glass Cutter   A glass-cutting tool shaped like a pencil, with a small wheel at one end used to secure the glass.

Glazing   Fitting, furnishing, or securing with glass.

Hinge   A small piece of paper that holds artwork in place. It can be made of various materials, including Japanese paper, liner tape, or pressure-sensitive tape.

Kraft Paper   Brown wrapping paper often used on the back of frames as a dust cover.

Kerf   The space of the cut made by a saw, ranging from slightly finer than 1/32 inch with a hand-powered saw to slightly thicker than 1/8 inch with a power saw. Considering kerf is important because it will indicate how much material will be lost in the sawing process.

Liner   An insert between the artwork and the frame opening (essentially a frame within a frame) that is used with oil painting on canvas and for a second or third mat when multiple mats are used.

Masonite   Fiberboard made from wood fibers.

Mat   A protective board around artwork that separates it from the glazing and usually enhances it.

Mat Board   A heavy paper board from which mats and backing boards are cut. It can be acid-free, 100-percent rag, or regular. Regular mat board has an acid-free core and backing, but the top colored paper can still be acidic.

Primary and secondary mats cut from mat board.

Mat Cutter A device which cuts the holes (windows) in mats. There are many brands of cutter. Your choice will depend on the amount of money you care to spend and the amount of convenience you require from the cutter.

Media The materials the art is made from. Common examples are oil, watercolor, pastel, acrylic, and charcoal.

Miter A joint formed by joining two pieces of wood at the corner of a picture frame.

Miter Box A tool used for sawing moldings at precise angles for a perfect fit at the corners of a picture frame. Once always used with a backsaw, miter boxes are now often motorized.

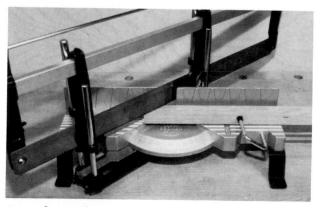

A metal miter box.

Miter Gauge The part of a table saw that slides in the miter slot of the saw.

Miter Vise A tool used for holding two pieces of framing wood as they're attached with glue and brads to form a corner.

Moldings Strips of wood used to make frames or the basic outsides of the frames. Home framers can use builders' moldings, framers' moldings, shop-made moldings, or combinations of the above.

Molding.

Mount To secure an object or artwork to a backboard using adhesive of some kind.

Nail Set A tool used to push a brad deeper than a hammer can reach. It usually has to be followed with nail-hole filler to disguise the nail holes in a picture frame.

Plexiglas A lightweight acrylic glazing especially useful for larger picture frames or when shipping picture frames. The material's electrostatic attraction can make it a dust magnet, so it is unsuitable for use with charcoal and like media.

Plywood A sheet material made by gluing together thin layers of wood.

Primary Mat The piece of mat board directly underneath the artwork that touches it.

Rabbet   A notch or dado on the inside edge of a wooden frame that holds all the parts of the artwork being framed.

Rag   A type of mat board. Rag is cloth converted to pulp for making paper. The finest mat boards are made of paper with a very high rag content.

Screw Eyes   Screws with small eyelets at one end that are used to attach the hanging wire to the back of the wooden frame.

Secondary Mat   The mat which is closer to the glass than the primary mat. While the primary mat is usually white, the secondary mat will often be a color.

Spacer   Material used to prevent artwork from touching the glass. It can be made of whatever is convenient, such as strips of wood, mat board, lath, or any commercial product designed for this use.

Squaring   Making sure that the parts of the picture frame form perfect right (90-degree) angles.

Substrate   The backboard of a picture frame.

Utility Knife   A tool with a replaceable blade used for cutting the outsides of mat board, fabric, and other material.

Utility knife.

Metric Equivalents

INCHES TO MILLIMETRES AND CENTIMETRES

MM—millimetres   *CM—centimetres*

Inches	MM	CM	Inches	CM	Inches	CM
⅛	3	0.3	9	22.9	30	76.2
¼	6	0.6	10	25.4	31	78.7
⅜	10	1.0	11	27.9	32	81.3
½	13	1.3	12	30.5	33	83.8
⅝	16	1.6	13	33.0	34	86.4
¾	19	1.9	14	35.6	35	88.9
⅞	22	2.2	15	38.1	36	91.4
1	25	2.5	16	40.6	37	94.0
1¼	32	3.2	17	43.2	38	96.5
1½	38	3.8	18	45.7	39	99.1
1¾	44	4.4	19	48.3	40	101.6
2	51	5.1	20	50.8	41	104.1
2½	64	6.4	21	53.3	42	106.7
2	76	7.6	22	55.9	43	109.2
3½	89	8.9	23	58.4	44	111.8
4	102	10.2	24	61.0	45	114.3
4½	114	11.4	25	63.5	46	116.8
5	127	12.7	26	66.0	47	119.4
6	152	15.2	27	68.6	48	121.9
7	178	17.8	28	71.1	49	124.5
8	203	20.3	29	73.7	50	127.0

INDEX

A

Adjustable Clamping Company pivoting jaw clamp, 29
Angle gauge, 114
"Antiquing," 51, 52
Artwork
assembling, 92–104, 121
as a component of picture frames, 15
protecting, 10, 11
Automatic tape gun, 76, 77, 79, 92, 94, 121
Awl, 33, 92

B

Backboard
as a component of picture frames, 15
definition of, 121
Backsaw, definition of, 121
Baroque frames, 37
Bartley's paste varnish, 50
Bessy band clamp, 29, 30
Bevel, definition of, 121
Bits, for routing molding profiles, 45, 46–47, 48, 49, 53, 54
Blades, sharpening and maintaining, 9
Blocking, definition of, 108, 121
"Bone," 31, 84
Bookmatching, 110
Brad, definition of, 121
Brad installer, 92
Bumpers, 95, 102, 104, 121

C

Carcass, definition of, 121
Cellux tape gun, 31
Chisel, 30, 31
Chop molding, 40, 121
Clamps, 25, 26–29, 30
Commercial picture frames
choosing, 36, 37, 40

disassembling, 40, 41, 42
for posters, 117
Complex moldings, making, 53, 54–55
Conservation glass, 87
Corner clamp, 121
Curved-opening mats, cutting, 79, 80–86

D

Dado
cutting a, 65, 66
definition of, 12
Design considerations for picture frames, 10–14
Double matting, 73, 74–78, 79
Dovetail saw, definition of, 121
Dry-mounting, 121
Dust collection, 43
Dust cover
as a component of picture frames, 15, 16
definition of, 121
Dust mask, 9

E

Easel backing, definition of, 121
Electric sander, 113, 115
Excel polyester glues, 30

F

Face shield, 9
Featherboard, 53
Filler
as a component of picture frames, 15
definition of, 121
Fillet, 121
Finishing
definition of, 122
frame stock, 56
molding, 50, 51–52, 53
project, 67

Firescreen, 109, 110–115, 116
Fletcher-Terry products
mat cutters, 69, 70–85
point drivers, 32, 33, 92, 93
Floating, definition of, 122
Foam-core board, 40, 109, 122
"Frameless" painting, 13, 14
Framer's molding, 122
Frames, picture
basic, cutting and assembling, 56–67, 68
burnishing, 121
commercial, 36, 37, 38, 40, 41, 42
definition of, 36
finishing, 65
open, 63, 64–67
Framing clamps
Adjustable Clamp Company clamp, 29
Bessy band clamp, 29, 30
Hirsch clamps, 27, 28
ProMan framing clamp set, 29, 30
Swanson Picture Framing Cut 'n' Clamp set, 27, 28
Ulmia spring miter clamp set, 28, 29
Wolfcraft clamps, 27, 28
Woodcraft Supply clamps, 25, 26, 27
Framing vise, 122
Freestanding needlework frame, 109, 110–115, 116

G

Garage sales, 40
Glass
as a component of picture frames, 41, 42
cutting, 87, 88–91, 96, 97, 98
definition of, 122
selecting, 87
washing, 96, 99
Glazing, definition of, 122

Glue, 30
Gorilla polyester glues, 30

H
Hanger hook, 65, 99
Hanger wire, 99, 100
Hearing protection, 43
Hexagonal frames, 30, 35
Hinge, definition of, 122
Hirsch clamp, 27, 28

J
Jeweler's file, 96, 97
Joiners, assembling wooden frame
    corners with, 60, 61–62, 63
Jointer/planer, 45
Jorgensen miter-cutting tools
    Clamp & Saw tool, 18
    Professional compound miter saw,
    18, 19
    six-angle miter box, 18

K
Kerf, definition of, 122
Kiln-dried stock, 44
Klingsor sanding sponge, 50, 51
Kraft paper, 92, 93, 94, 122

L
Lathe, 109, 110
Liner, definition of, 122
Lion Miter-Trimmer, 21, 22
Logan mat cutter, 81

M
Makita miter-cutting tools, 22, 23, 24
Masonite, 13, 14, 122
Mat
    definition of, 122
    types of, 68, 69
Mat board
    as a component of picture frames,
    15
    choosing and cutting, 68–86
    definition of, 10, 68, 122
Mat cutters, 69, 70–72, 73, 122
Media, definition of, 122
Metal frames, assembling, 95, 96–
    104
Mineral glass, 87
Miter boxes
    cutting metal frames with, 96
    cutting stock with, 56
    definition of, 122
    maintenance techniques, 25
    Makita, 22, 23, 24
    safety instructions for, 24, 25

Miter clamp, 121
Miter gauge
    definition of, 122
    on a table saw, 44, 56
Miters
    cutting, 65, 66
    definition of, 122
    tools for cutting, 17, 18–24, 25
Miter saw, definition of, 121
Miter vase, definition of, 122
Moldings
    chop, 121
    commercial, 36–39, 40
    definition of, 10, 122
    making, 43–55
    for picture frame projects, 117
Mount, definition of, 122

N
Nailset, 31, 32, 122
Needlework, framing, 13, 108–115,
    116
Nobex miter-cutting tools
    Champion 180 miter saw, 19, 20
    ProMan miter saw, 19, 20
Nonglare glass, 87, 120

O
Octagonal frames, 30, 35

P
Panel retainers. See turnbuttons
Paste varnish, 50, 51
Pentagonal frames, 13, 35
Picture frames
    adding a finish to, 52, 53
    burnishing, 92
    designs for, 10–14, 40, 41, 42
    with easy access to items, 63
    glass for, 87–91
    hanging, 105, 107
    refinishing, 40
    stock for, determining amount of,
    34–45
    tools for making, 17–35
Picture framing
    definition of, 8
    steps in, 8
    tools for, 17–35
Picture hanger, 65
Plastic-scoring knife, 69
Plexiglas
    cutting, 117, 118
    definition of, 123
    used in picture frames, 11, 12, 90,
    91

Plywood, definition of, 123
Point driver, 31, 32
Polyester glue, 30
Polyvinyl acetate glues, 30
Poster frame project, 12, 116, 117–
    118
Power tools
    band saw, 113, 114
    joiners, 61, 62, 63
    jointer/planer, 45
    lathe, 110, 111
    miter trimmer, 21–22, 58
    motorized miter saws, 17, 22–24,
    25
    table saw, 43, 44, 45, 49, 50, 53,
    54, 55, 65, 66, 113, 114
    using, 9
Primary mat
    cutting, 69
    definition of, 73, 123
Projects
    needlework project, 108–115, 116
    poster frame project, 116, 117–
    118
ProMan framing clamp set, 29, 30
Push stick, 53
Putty, 52, 53

R
Rabbet
    cutting a, 49, 50, 56
    definition of, 123
Rag board, definition of, 123
Random orbit sander, 30
Rectangular frames, 35
Router, cutting profiles with, 45,
    46–49, 53, 54
Rub 'n' Buff paint product, 51, 52
Ruler, 31

S
Safety glasses, 9
Safety instructions for power tools
    general, 9
    for using miter boxes, 24, 25
Sanders
    detail, 56, 57
    drum, 115
    random orbit, 30
Sandpaper
    as a tool
    sanding mats with, 75, 76, 82, 83,
    84
    sanding molding with, 50, 51
Screen stock, 65
Screwdriver, 64

Screw eyes, 33, 123
Secondary mat
    cutting, 76, 77–78, 79
    definition of, 69, 123
Skew-angle chisel, 30, 31
Spacer, definition of, 123
Spray finishes, 52, 53
Spring clamps, 58, 63
Square (noun), 31, 105
Square (verb) 123
Stanley hand knife, 117, 118
Stop blocks, 57
Straightedge, 31
Substrate, definition of, 123
Swanson Picture Framing Cut 'n'
    Clamp set, 27, 28

T
Table saw
    cutting dadoes with a, 65, 66

cutting stock with a, 43, 44, 45, 53,
    54, 55
flattening feet with a, 113, 114
sawing rabbets on a, 49, 50
Tape gun, 31
Tools
    awl, 33
    "bone," 31
    chisel, 30, 31
    clamps, 25, 26–29, 30
    drill and bit, 31, 32
    glue, 30
    miter-cutting, 17, 18–24, 25
    nail set, 31, 32
    point driver, 32, 33
    ruler, 31
    screw eyes, 33
    square, 31
    straightedge, 31
    utility knife, 32, 33, 69, 123

wall hangers, 33
wire, 33
TrackMaster, 107
Turnbuttons, 64, 111, 113, 116

U
Ulmia spring miter clamp set, 28, 29
Utility knife, 32, 33, 69, 123

V
Varnish, for molding, 50, 51

W
Wall hangers, 33
Waxpaper, 64
Window glass, 87
Wire, 33
Wire cutter, 92, 95
Wolfcraft clamps, 27, 28